Create a Quilt

Joyce Mori

KRAUSE PUBLICATIONS
700 East State St., Iola, WI 54990-0001
Telephone (715) 445-2214
www.krause.com

Please call or write for our free catalog of publications. Our toll-free number to place an order or obtain a free catalog is 800-258-0929 or please use our regular business telephone 715-445-2214 for editorial comment and further information.

Manufactured in the United States of America

Library of Congress Cataloging-In-Publication Data

Mori, Joyce
Create a quilt

1. Quilting   2. Sewing   3. Title

ISBN 0-87341-620-1

98-87357
CIP

Acknowledgments

Thanks so much to Anastasia Pavlovic and Theresa Fleming for designing blocks to use in this book. Delores Stemple worked very quickly to complete the quilting on some of the quilts. And I appreciate her perfect quilting stitches. Barbara Pavlovic helped by finishing the quilting on a quilt designed by her granddaughter. Pat Hill, my special friend from California, designed blocks and made quilts for this book.

I appreciate the wonderful fabrics supplied by Demetria Zahoudanis of RJR Fabrics. I enjoyed using them in several wall quilts. Linda and Dean Moran of Marble T Design (3391 South Nastar Dr., Tucson, AZ 85730) provided lovely hand marbled fabrics used in some of the blocks.

Eric Merrill did a wonderful job on all the diagrams in this book. He had to translate my primitive graphic designs into clear and attractive designs.

My editor, Barbara Case, is terrific. She makes sure I don't leave anything out and that everything is easily understood by the readers.

As always, my special thanks and appreciation go to my husband John who helps me over creative blocks and color selection difficulties. He has adapted very well to being married to a dedicated quilter and writer. I thank him for allowing me to do something I enjoy.

Table of Contents

Introduction

All quilters have been to quilt shows or seen pictures in a magazine where the notation for the quilt stated that the design was an original by Susie Q. Quilter. You probably think it must be very difficult to create an original design. You may feel you would never be able to design such a quilt, and you assume that Susie Q. must be an artist by training. Erase these thoughts. I'm going to show you how easy and fun it is to design original blocks and quilts.

We all tend to be intimidated by the term "original design." This book has been written to show you that it's really as easy as child's play to create an original design—whether it be a block, a small quilt, or a full size quilt. No special art or design skills are needed.

If you follow the step-by-step ideas in this book, *you will create original quilts as easily as you sew quilts from patterns*. At the end of the book are a series of design pages containing over 100 individual design elements to manipulate to create blocks and quilts. Some of these elements are as basic as triangles, squares, and rectangles. Other elements are built up from these basic units into shapes not usually seen by quilters. These beyond-the-basic elements come from art and craft work of artisans from cultures all over the world. I have adapted them to fit the needs of quilters and to provide quilters with some new elements to use in design.

With the system taught in this book, *you don't have to draw any design elements yourself*. They are provided for you. All the design units are drawn to the same scale. You cut them out and move them around on a piece of grid paper to create your design. Your entire family can sit at the table and design with you.

This designing technique is relaxing and fun. The combinations are almost limitless, so no two quilters

will create the same design. You will create your own unique and attractive quilt.

No expensive equipment is required. You don't need a computer and printer, but if you have access to and use computer drawing programs, you can use them in the design process if you wish. You'll find computer options throughout the book.

Of course, it would be useless to design quilts easily if these quilts could not then be sewn together easily. You'll learn how to look at a design to see the way the elements can be sewn together. Many of the units can be quickly cut with a rotary cutter and plastic ruler.

This is a book for beginning designers, but the techniques taught will be useful for advanced designers as well. You can progress from very simple designs to more complex ones. And you can use simple design strategies and move to more complex designing options.

Let's get started on your journey toward an understanding of how to design an original quilt. I encourage you to use and modify any of my designs or the designs of the guest designers. However, please give proper credit to the original designer.

Joyce Mori

Chapter 1

The Basic Technique

As you read this book, you will see many examples of quilts and blocks created with my designing technique. These examples are rendered in actual fabrics and in shaded illustrations. The examples quickly show you that the blocks you create are suitable for everyone's favorite fabrics and colors. For each design strategy, I show you only enough designs so you understand the technique and see a sample of the range of designs possible. I don't want to overload you with designs that might influence how you proceed with your creative adventure in designing. I know from the results I've seen in my classes that just as soon as I think I know every way some design units can be combined to create a quilt or block, my students surprise me and create something else. That is creativity!

The Basic Designing Method

The concept starts with the design elements on pages 110 to 122. You will copy them, cut them out, and move them around on a piece of graph paper to create a pleasing quilt design or block. Surprisingly, this is faster than working at a computer, though I give you instances where you can use a computer drawing program if you have one. The technique is so simple a child can do it, but the various design strategies provide ideas that work for beginning to advanced quilters. You will begin to create original quilt blocks within minutes of sitting down to work.

I've found that other books on design, while interesting, often require that I carefully read and reread the directions before beginning. I simply don't want to take the time to do that. I want a plug-and-play format, so to speak. I want satisfying results and I want a technique that will quickly break a creative block. (As you might have guessed, I am a Mac person. You don't need a degree in computer science to use that computer successfully. I find my MacIntosh computer to be intuitive and that's how I hope my design method works for you.)

As you read each chapter and complete the exercises, you will be amazed at what you can accomplish with this technique. Sit down with your children and do this together. Use one or two exercises as a guild workshop. Work on designing while watching TV. Once you get started, you won't want to stop.

Supplies

Rubber cement
Pencil
Eraser
Ruler
Zip lock plastic bag or small, clear, plastic box to hold loose design units
Scissors
Wite-Out®
Colored pencils—light gray, medium gray, black
5 file folders
Temporary spray adhesive (optional but very helpful)
Tweezers
Sheet of transparent grid template plastic - 1/4" grid
Glue

Before you begin to design, carefully cut out the design pages, graph paper page, and block pages at the end of the book and take them to your copy store. Try to use the same store and same brand of machine so any distortion that might occur will remain consistent.

Make the following copies:

Grid graph page - 10 copies on regular paper, 2 copies on card stock
Grid block pages - 6 copies of each page on regular paper, 2 copies of each on card stock
Designing element pages - 10 copies of each page on regular paper, 5 copies of each on card stock
Line drawing element pages - 10 copies of each page on regular paper
Optional: If you want to design with the blocks in the block gallery section, make at least 4 copies of each page. This allows you to try 4-block setting arrangements.

Card stock is used for business cards. It usually doubles the cost of copying, but having the designs, grid graph page, and grid block pages on card stock makes the elements easier to move around on the graph page or grid block page and more durable. You use your cardboard versions of the design elements only for designing purposes. The paper design elements will eventually be cut out and glued down on the paper grid graph page. As you continue to design, you will have to make more copies of the element pages on regular weight paper.

The design elements and graph paper are all based on the scale of four squares to the inch. This makes a size that is easy to see. I usually designate that one square equals one inch in the completed project. There will be more discussion of this in Chapter 3.

Before You Begin

Use file folders to store the copied and original pages so you keep everything separate. Label the folders as follows.
- ❀ Original pages cut out of this book
- ❀ Design element pages copied on regular paper
- ❀ Design element pages copied on card stock
- ❀ Graph grid pages and graph block pages copied on regular paper
- ❀ Graph grid pages and graph block pages copied on card stock

Cut out the separate design elements. You can do this while watching TV or listening to music. It takes less than an hour to cut out the starter elements. (The starter elements are any basic shapes you decide to work with. Select several sizes of squares, triangles, and rectangles as your starter elements for learning the basic design process.) Since you do the designing with the card stock elements, cut those out first and keep them in a box or bag to be reused every time you sit down to design. Cut out only one page of each card stock design page

(this will give you enough elements to work with without filling your design table with extra pieces). Cut them out carefully on the outside of the element line. If you need more elements for a design repeat or if you and a friend are designing together, cut out extra elements from the other pages.

For a quick start, cut out only a few elements—some squares, triangles, and rectangles. Select some different sizes. As you look at the individual motifs, you will see that there are some units that are mirror images of each other. You need mirror image elements to develop designs such as the traditional Pigeon Toes Block.

Figure 1-1 Mirror image elements.

Figure 1-2 Pigeon Toes block.

Designing a Quilt Block

Let's begin the design process by creating an original quilt block. Lay a **card stock grid block page** in front of you. Notice that the blocks have sizes under them. This gives you a general idea of the size block you are creating. You can make other size blocks by using only portions of these blocks or by using the grid graph page without specific block outlines on it. If you use a grid graph page, arrange your elements and draw a block outline around the arrangement you design to form the block unit. You can also draw an outline of the size block you want to create and then fill in that area with design elements.

Helpful Hint

Spray the card stock grid block page with a temporary spray adhesive such as Sullivan's Basting Spray or ATP 505 to keep the design elements from moving once you place them down. Before spraying, paper clip two 3″ by 11″ pieces of scrap paper to the outside edges of the grid page, leaving the grid block units exposed. Spray the adhesive on the grid blocks and remove the scrap paper. The grid blocks will have a tacky surface but the area around the blocks is not sticky. You'll need to respray after you've used the page for a great deal of designing or after a few weeks. When you've finished designing, cover the sticky page with a piece of waxed paper to protect it.

To begin the design process, lay your cutout card stock elements face up in front of you on the table just like you'd do before starting a jigsaw puzzle. There are two easy ways to approach designing a quilt block. Read through the two options and decide which feels most comfortable for your first design.

Option #1 - Designing a Block Using Squares, Triangles, and Rectangles

These are the geometric units that quilters are most familiar with, so it may be easiest for you to start with these basic units. Don't assume that every block using these basic units has already been designed. Even if you create something that is already a block drawn elsewhere, you have created

it on your own and you can learn ways to modify it to make it original.

Select some basic units and place them inside one of the block grids. Add other triangles, squares, or rectangles to fill in the space. For your first attempts, use design pieces in the size range illustrated below.

Figure 1-3

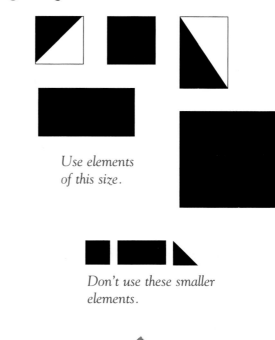

Use elements of this size.

Don't use these smaller elements.

Helpful Hint

You may find it helpful to use a pair of tweezers to lift up and place the design elements on your blocks. Another helpful tool is Puzzle Pal, a device that resembles a pen with a tiny suction cup on its end that allows you to pick up and place pieces of a puzzle or, in this case, design elements. If you didn't spray the card stock grid block page with temporary adhesive, you may find it easy to move the pieces into the block with the eraser end of a wooden pencil.

Study the illustrations in Figure 1-4 to see how these basic design units were used to create quilt blocks. You might find it helpful to actually re-create these designs. Once you have placed the pieces on your block grid, move them around to

Create a Quilt

make a new design with the same motifs I used or add one other design element to the mix.

I have no idea if these blocks have already been designed by someone else. If they interest you, keep them in your file. You might use them as is or combine them with other blocks or use them as a starting medallion for a wall quilt (more about these options later).

When you have a pleasing design, cut out the elements you used from the regular paper pages and glue them to a regular paper block grid page with rubber cement. You now have a permanent record of your original creations! Wow! See how easy it is to create a block.

Now that you understand the basic design technique, it is time to provide you with some design strategies to help you create attractive and original quilt blocks. You can now use the smaller design elements.

Design Strategy - The Importance of White Space and Lack of Symmetry

The illustrations are shown in black and white so your perception of the design won't be affected by color. The black and white contrast allows you to easily visualize which parts of the design are emphasized—the black. You will see examples of the blocks made up in fabrics interspersed throughout the book.

In Figure 1-5, notice how the blocks are designed with only squares and rectangles, both very common units, yet the blocks look (and probably are) very original. The reason they look so different is because of the uneven amounts of white space separating the individual units. The blocks are also asymmetrical (both halves are not equal) which makes it more likely that they're original.

These block illustrations don't include grid lines. Grid lines are omitted from most of the illustrations in the book to help you better visualize a design without distracting lines. You will need to have grid lines on your drawings to help you understand how to cut and sew a block (see Chapter 8).

Please don't look at these blocks and assume that you'll never make them because they are so nontraditional. Look at pages 16 and 17 for some very nontraditional blocks sewn in very traditional fabrics.

To see more ideas for this strategy (which is somewhat unusual for most quilters), study the windows designed by Frank Lloyd Wright and other members of the Prairie School of Architecture.

Figure 1-4

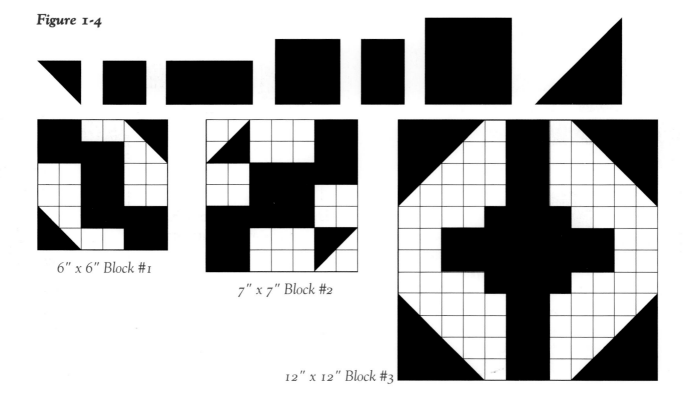

6" x 6" Block #1

7" x 7" Block #2

12" x 12" Block #3

Figure 1-5 ❀ *Design strategy—white space and lack of symmetry.*

Figure 1-6 ❀ *Design strategy—simplify.*

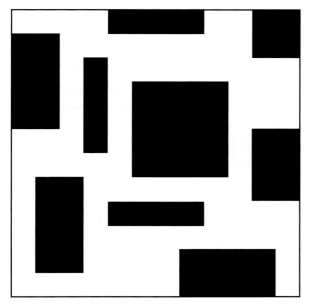

12″ x 12″ Block #4

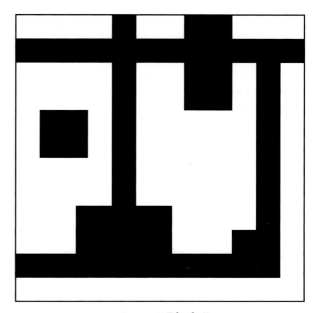

12″ x 12″ Block #7

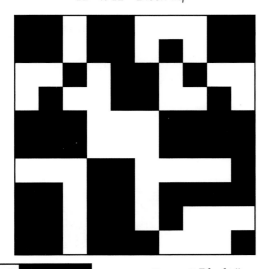

10″ x 10″ Block #5

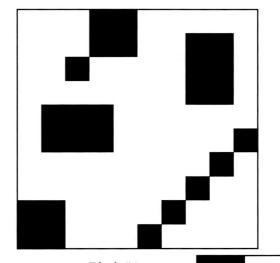

10″ x 10″ Block #8

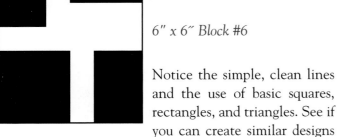

6″ x 6″ Block #6

6″ x 6″ Block #9

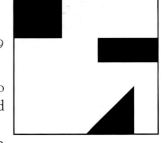

Notice the simple, clean lines and the use of basic squares, rectangles, and triangles. See if you can create similar designs by thinking "less" instead of more, simple rather than complex. If you want a more complex looking design, you can use many colors in the design. If you are a more advanced quilter, you can consider

adding narrow strips of fabric to your design to imitate stained glass leading.

Look at the work of Dutch artist Piet Mondrian for more ideas on the effective graphic use of simple geometric shapes. Study Figure 1-6 above to see blocks that illustrate this strategy of simple, not complex.

Option #2 - Designing a Block Using Other Elements

Select one or two of the nonbasic units—elements that are more complex. These elements have been built up by joining squares, rectangles, and/or triangles together. Some will not be familiar to you, but a block created with them will likely be original. Be sure you have multiple copies of each unit. Include the mirror image of any selected elements if necessary (see Figure 1-1).

Put four elements together to create a block. Turn the elements different ways. Study Figure 1-7 for examples of quilt blocks created by combining four of a nonbasic element from page 117. Some of the elements are mirror-image versions. Isn't this fantastic? I told you designing original quilts was easy.

Design Strategy - The Nonsquare Block

Dismantle one of the square blocks you have created and put it together again on the grid graph page, not the grid block page. This time, change the relationships between the elements so the block becomes rectangular instead of square (see Figure 1-8). This will probably mean pushing some elements together more and/or spreading some out. You will create a new version of the block, probably one that is very original since quilters tend to rely on the square block format even though our beds are rectangular and it would make more sense to use rectangular blocks!

You have now created some block designs. You have glued your paper design elements onto a paper grid page or paper grid block page. You can cut out the block designs and glue them all onto a plain piece of paper. This will allow you to put more blocks on a single piece of paper. Chapter 2 tells you how to use these blocks as a basis for your next quilt.

Figure 1-7

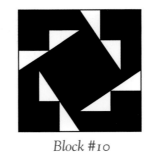

Block #10

A series of blocks created with a nonbasic element. Reduced in size.

Block #11

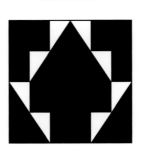

Actual size design element

Figure 1-8 ❀ *Design strategy—the nonsquare block.*

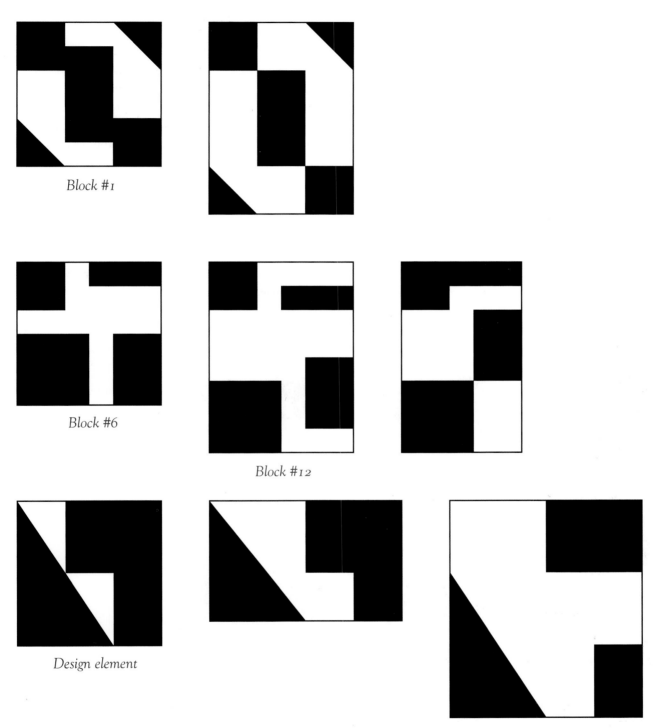

Block #1

Block #6

Block #12

Design element

Block #1 (12" x 12"). Four blocks
are combined and the resulting design
creates diagonal lines.

Block #1 (12" x 12"). Four blocks are rotated and
combined for this unit, creating a whirlwind motif.

(12" x 20"). Two
#39 blocks are com-
bined to create this
larger block.

(10" x 10"). The red mar-
bled fabric in this block is
supplied by Marble T
Design, Tucson, Ariz. It
combines beautifully with a
petroglyph print. This is
Block #50 modified.

(12" x 12"). Four
#6 blocks are
combined to form
this unit.

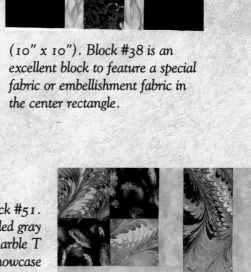

(10" x 10"). Block #38 is an excellent block to feature a special fabric or embellishment fabric in the center rectangle.

(12" x 12"). This is a variation of Block #15. The block is created by combining four design elements. More possibilities exist for combinations of this design element and its mirror image.

(8" x 8"). Block #51. A beautiful marbled gray fabric from Marble T Design is the showcase fabric in this block.

(8" x 8"). A wonderful rust marble fabric from Marble T Designs is used in Block #59. Scrap fabrics could also be used effectively in this block.

(8" x 10"). Block #18 features marble fabric from Marble T Designs. This block has wonderful diagonal movement and some exciting designs can be created to take advantage of this feature

Chapter 2

Designing a Wall Quilt

*I*n the previous chapter, you learned to create unique and attractive quilt blocks. In fact, if you are like me, once you start designing, it is very hard to stop. There is always one more idea to explore. However, once you have accumulated a series of blocks, it's time to learn how to use those blocks in quilt designs.

To create a wall quilt design with your blocks, you need multiple copies of the blocks. The next time you go out to do errands, stop at the copy store and make at least four copies of the pages that contain your block designs. Once you have four copies of each block, you can begin to play with arrangements for them.

Helpful Hint

Some blocks look best when laid out in nine-block or more arrangements instead of four-block sets, but to start, you may not want to make nine copies of the pages. After studying how four blocks look together, decide if you like the arrangement. At that point, you may wish to make additional copies of the blocks so you can try some nine-block arrangements or even up to 36-block arrangements.

Helpful Hint

If you have a computer drawing program, you can draw your original new blocks on a page. Group the block and make duplicates of it. Follow the arrangement strategies discussed below to create a wall quilt. In this age of computers, I still find it much quicker to move the cardboard elements around on the grid page for the actual designing process. For me, it's a much easier way to try new combinations of elements, to remove elements, to rotate elements, etc. I believe I work faster without the computer. And obviously, many quilters don't have a computer and/or drawing program. But I do find it desirable to work with the actual block in the drawing program once I've created the block with my technique.

Creating a Wall Quilt

Option #1 - Four-Block Sets or Repeating Blocks

I have used some of the blocks created in Chapter 1 for the various strategies in this chapter. I believe this is the best way to illustrate the versatility of the blocks and this designing technique.

Many of your favorite antique and modern quilts consist of designs that are repetitions of a single block. Sometimes new designs are formed at the intersections of the blocks. Likewise, the final coloring of the quilt of repeating blocks can determine its beauty as a final project. Chapter 6 will go into more detail on coloring options.

Study Figure 2-1 carefully. Four blocks from Chapter 1 were combined in various ways. Notice the change in position of the little white circle. The circle was added so you could follow the variations in orientation of each block. Sometimes the circle appears in the four outside corners, sometimes it appears in the center of the arrangements, and other times the position is varied.

Now look at Figures 2-2 and 2-3. Here you see another block from Chapter 1 and some of its possible arrangements. Not all blocks form attractive or interesting configurations in all format variations. Play around and decide on ones that are useful and appealing to you. You probably notice that some designs show strong diagonal lines and others illustrate a rotational movement. Some designs form enclosed areas at their center or form an interesting design at the center point.

The next step is to determine how these four-block units look when combined with more of the same block units. Try nine-, 16-, and 36-block combinations. Figure 2-4 shows a 16-block arrangement. One of the four-block units in Figure 2-2 showed the possibility of diagonal lines and that four-block combination created this 16-block quilt design. There is a very strong diagonal component to the design and careful selection of colors would really emphasize that.

Figure 2-5 shows a nine-block arrangement of an asymmetric block. This combination creates a design with the potential for strong horizontal lines. To really explore the possibilities of your separate blocks, combine them in at least four-block arrangements.

I'm sure some very original quilt designs will appear in front of you. However, even if you feel a block doesn't work in your four-block arrangement,

don't discard it. Keep it in your file. There can be other uses for blocks as you will see as you read further in this book.

Figure 2-6 shows what happens when you repeat a four-block sequence to create a 36-block arrangement. The four-block unit was given a simple repeat nine times. If you look carefully at the design, you will see on-point squares, whirlwinds, and stepped squares. The coloring of the design will help you isolate certain interesting design elements.

In Figure 2-7, you probably see a complex quilt design. At first glance, you might think that all kinds of blocks were created to achieve this quilt. However, when you break the design down, you see that only two different four-block units were used. In each corner of the design is that wonderful diagonal combination created in Figure 2-2 and used again in Figure 2-4. Simple enough. The diagonal nature of the design helps to focus attention to the center area of the quilt. The other five four-block units are really one of the other four-block combinations from Figure 2-2. This is a 36-

Figure 2-1

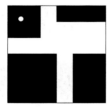

6" x 6" Block #6
Notice the location of the white dot. This illustrates the change in orientation of the block.

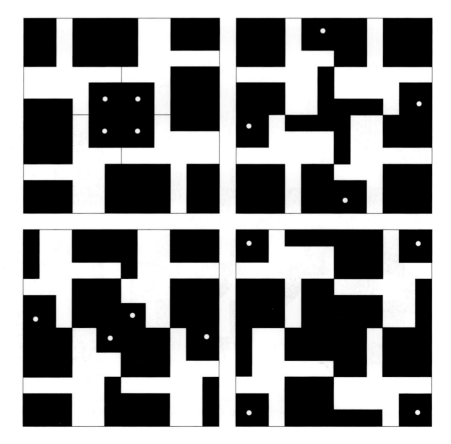

Figure 2-2

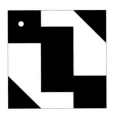

6" x 6" Block #1

Figure 2-3

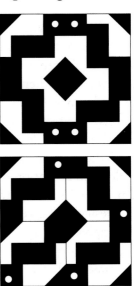

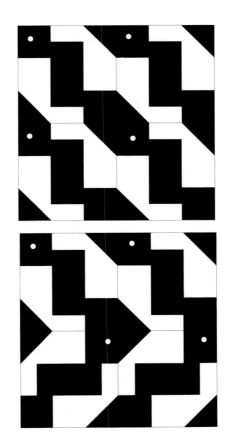

Figure 2-4

One of the arrangements of blocks in Figure 2-2 showed the possibility of the diagonal line. This 16-block arrangement shows a strong sense of movement in the design, which is very attractive.

Figure 2-5

This is a nine-block arrangement. It is not symmetrical, but it is still a workable design. Asymmetric blocks can result in interesting designs when used in nine-block formats.

Figure 2-6

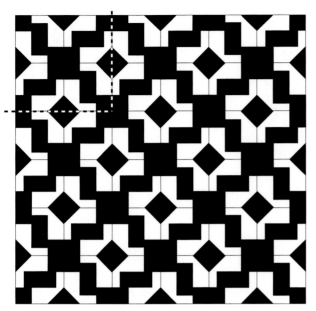

This 36-block arrangement features a repeat of one of the four-block units of Figure 2-2. Notice there are several new designs that could be isolated with the proper use of color. There are whirlwinds and stepped squares.

Figure 2-7

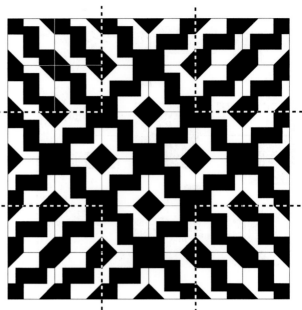

This 36-block arrangement takes advantage of the diagonal line that was revealed in the multiple-block arrangement in Figure 2-4. The blocks are placed in each corner so the diagonal lines point toward the quilt's center. Then a second block from Figure 2-4 is used for the remaining five blocks in the quilt. If you look carefully at this illustration, you will see several emerging geometric sections of the quilt that could be isolated by coloring them in different ways.

block quilt made of only two different four-block combinations.

There are so many ways to color this design. You can emphasize the diagonal lines or the central interlocking stepped squares or the light interior whirlwinds or only the larger dark squares. When you create a design that is visually appealing and that allows you to color it in many different ways, you have created a very successful quilt design.

Up to this point, I have shown examples of repeating blocks featuring only square blocks. What about the rectangular blocks you designed? Can you use those? Yes, but they are more difficult to work with. Square blocks are easy to manipulate because all the sides are equal. Rectangular blocks have unequal sides, so if you have a block and one next to it that has been turned 90 degrees, they don't match up along the joining sides. This means you may need to add filler units. See Figure 2-8 for an example of rectangular blocks and the filler unit

needed. Notice the placement of the white dot. Check Figure 2-1 to see how different the square block looks with that format compared to the rectangular variation of the block. The rectangular block is not identical to the square version. There is more white space and the units are moved around in the extra space to achieve balance.

If a rectangular block has a long side that is double the short side, it can be easier to join multiple units. Figure 2-9 shows two options.

I encourage you to make copies of the pages that show the four-block units or multiple-block designs. You can cut the units apart and work with them as you would your own quilt blocks. Due to space limitations, I have not explored all the possibilities for the block designs presented in this book, so feel free to work them and develop unique arrangements and wall quilt designs.

Figure 2-8

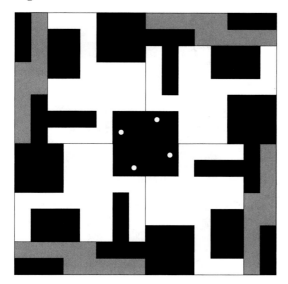

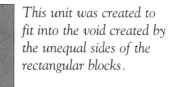 This unit was created to fit into the void created by the unequal sides of the rectangular blocks.

Rectangular block used in the design.

Design created with four blocks plus the narrow filler unit.

Figure 2-9

Four units, 16 blocks combined with a center unit in each four-block set.

 The rectangular block. The long side is twice as long as the short side.

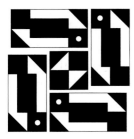 *The layout of the four blocks. When the four blocks are combined, the center is a hole, so other units are placed inside.*

A wall quilt design produced from 32 rectangular blocks. Notice that a border-like design of rectangles appears. There is also a center pinwheel.

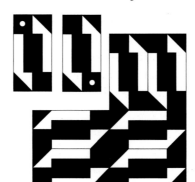 *Two rectangular blocks can be combined to create a square block.*

Option #2 - Combining Blocks

So far, you've probably been creating blocks rather randomly (unless you're a Type-A personality). Hopefully, you've designed some blocks that are the same size. If you don't have three or four blocks that are the same size, design some blocks to fill in size gaps. For instance, create three or four 6" blocks and three or four 12" blocks. That will allow you to try the ideas presented in this section.

Just as you can create an attractive quilt by repeating blocks, you can create an equally attractive quilt by combining two or three blocks and repeating those.

This design strategy can be less predictable than the repeating block strategy. To have blocks that will successfully work together, they need to share several characteristics.

❖ They should be the same size or related in size. For instance, 6" blocks can work with 12" blocks because four 6" blocks placed together create a 12" block.

❖ It's difficult to work with rectangular blocks unless they are the same size. Even then, rectangular blocks present more challenges than square blocks, but these can be resolved much as you dealt with the rectangular blocks in the previous section.

❖ It helps to use blocks together that have some similar design elements in the corners or along the sides. For instance, if one block has 2" squares in the corners and another has 2" triangles in the corners, they will likely work together. Where the corners meet, there will be matches. This is not a hard and fast rule. Figure 2-10 features a design where this is only partially true. Study the corners to see how the elements meet.

Figure 2-10

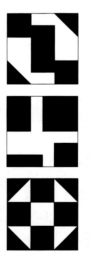

This quilt illustration has three blocks. Two of them were used in earlier designs in this chapter. The center block is created from elements found in the other two blocks and is needed to provide symmetry and balance for the wall quilt design.

In Chapter 4, you will learn that you can modify block combinations if the arrangement doesn't seem right, but for now, work with the blocks you have. Figure 2-11 shows the squares of the 6″ block meeting the narrow rectangles of the 12″ block. As long as the points where the sides or corners meet create a pleasing design feature, the resulting pattern can be effective.

Trust your visual acuity to determine if a design is pleasing and don't hesitate to ask a quilting friend for their opinion. Don't throw away a design because it appears slightly wrong. Many times, as you create additional blocks or begin to understand the other design strategies in this book, you will be able to rework a design and make it very attractive. As a quilter, you know you are subject to frequent bursts of inspiration—often in the middle of the night!

Option #3 - Dividing Blocks and Adding Sashing

Often blocks can be divided into sections. Such sections can be the half division of the block as in Figure 2-12. These half-block units are placed around all the edges of the four-block unit to create a border. However, you could use this entire design and repeat it as you would combine a series of four-block units. Also remember that these half-block units might work as an effective border or other design elements in quilt designs that didn't make use of the original block at all. You have, in effect, created a set of new design elements that are simply more complex than a basic square or rectangle.

In addition to dividing a block exactly in half, you can divide it where you see a natural division between the elements in the block. In Figure 2-13, the block could have been divided in thirds. I tried that but preferred the half division arrangement, even though it meant cutting the rectangle in half. I also divided the block in half again to create a quarter-block section.

As you become more accustomed to this design method, you can divide a block in half diagonally. You can then recombine the block or use the diagonal section in an on-point design. All you need is a pair of scissors and you are on your way to new designs.

Figure 2-11

In this design, a 6″ block is combined with a 12″ block. Since four 6″ blocks will fit inside a 12″ block, they can often be combined together. Five 12″ blocks are used in this quilt design. If you remove the center 12″ block and substitute four 6″ blocks, another lovely design is created.

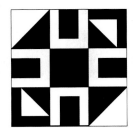

Figure 2-12

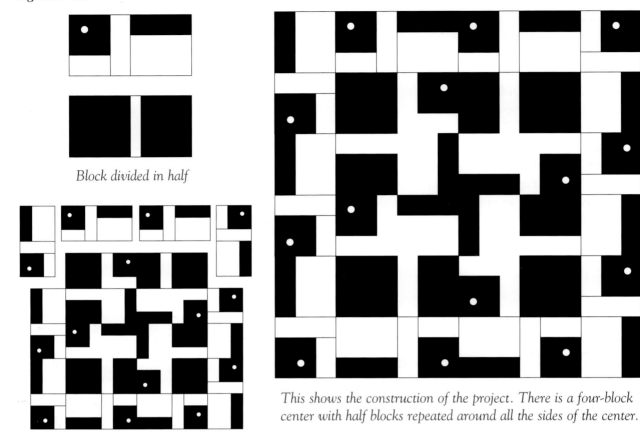

Block divided in half

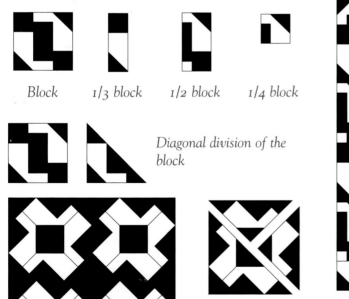

This shows the construction of the project. There is a four-block center with half blocks repeated around all the sides of the center.

Figure 2-13

Block   1/3 block   1/2 block   1/4 block

Diagonal division of the block

Sixteen diagonal blocks combined

Four diagonal blocks combined

This wall quilt shows a quarter block placed in each corner of the design. Half blocks are placed along the top, bottom, and sides of the quilt. The center of the quilt consists of a four-block unit taken from Figure 2-2.

Adding sashing is another strategy to try with the blocks you create. Adding sashing can break up the design. If you compare the top right block in Figure 2-1 with Figure 2-14, you can quickly see this principle. The pinwheel formed with dark rectangles where the four blocks meet is interrupted by the sashing and becomes less distinct.

Likewise, Figure 2-15 shows how the insertion of sashing between each block breaks up the diagonal line movement across the design. Compare Figure 2-15 with Figure 2-4. Of course, sashing adds size to your project, so you'll need fewer blocks to complete a quilt.

The sashing in these examples is plain. Remember, you can also make sashing with a pattern in it. With such a decorative sashing, you can reinforce or add to a design.

I'm guessing that by now your laundry is piled up, the garden needs weeding, and the family has eaten fast food or carryout for several days. You are having so much fun designing! You're probably wondering why you ever thought it was difficult to create original quilt designs. Seriously, I hope you are having fun with this. Designing your own quilt should not be intimidating. It should be fun, easy, and satisfying.

Figure 2-14

Sashing has been added to this four-block unit. Look at Figure 2-1 to see the unit with sashing.

Figure 2-15

Sashing has been added to the blocks from Figure 2-4. Notice that the diagonal movement has been interrupted, though it is still prominent.

Option #4 - Mirror Imaging

Back in Chapter 1, I explained the concept of mirror imaging. There is no reason not to try to mirror image an entire block. Go back to your grid sheet and move the elements around until you create a mirror image of a favorite block. Figure 2-16 shows one of the blocks and its mirror image. Look what happens when you combine the original block with its mirror image and then repeat those two blocks to produce a 16-block design. Notice that the white circle appears in this design so you can see how the two-block unit was flipped. The resulting design is very unlike the previous designs created with that block.

Figure 2-16

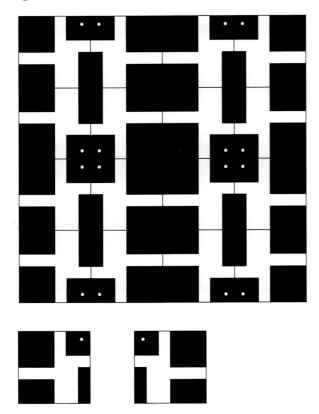

The block on the left is the original block created in Chapter 1. The block on the right is its mirror image. The wall quilt design was constructed with the original block and its mirror image.

Option #5 - On-Point Blocks

Up to now, the designs you've created use blocks in a normal, straight arrangement. But as a quilter, you know there is an arrangement format called "on-point" where a block is rotated 90 degrees. When the block is rotated, placed on-point, triangle units must be added on each side to create a regular square design (see Figure 2-17).

Try turning your blocks to achieve an on-point orientation. Sometimes the blocks look more interesting when turned this way. Actually, designing on-point blocks can be a more difficult concept to work with on graph paper, so I don't recommend it for your first projects.

In Figure 2-18, notice that the original block turned on-point doesn't fit within the grid lines of the grid graph paper. Notice the two triangles. On the left is the triangle of the original block. On the right is the type of triangle needed to fit on the graph paper when the block is turned on-point. They are different. Thus, to convert a block to be on-point and still fit the grid graph page, you must use different size elements.

I haven't supplied design elements that can be used on-point. The design elements aren't drawn to fit on the grid correctly in an on-point mode. That's why actually designing blocks on-point can be difficult. This is how I suggest you approach on-point settings. If you have a four-block unit that appeals to you, turn the paper so the design is on-point. Does it still look appealing to you? If it does, redraw the block on grid paper so it fits in an on-point setting. This is not difficult, but it does take

Figure 2-17

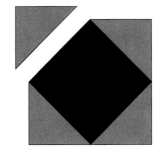

Square block.

Triangles added on each side to re-create a normal square block.

extra time and some planning. Remember, the sizes of the elements will change from the original. Then make copies and put the units together. You can then place, and probably glue, the quilt drawing onto grid graph page and draw in appropriate corner fill units to complete the design. I followed that procedure in Figure 2-18.

Figure 2-18

Five blocks (one is in the center) put together and corner triangles added. Grid lines are drawn in part of the design to show how the design is created.

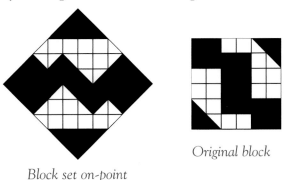

Block set on-point

Original block

These two elements aren't the same size. To keep the design elements on the grid lines, a different triangle must be used for the on-point version of the block.

Option #6 - Large Blocks as Setting Ideas

In this design strategy, you don't design a block per se, you design a set format for blocks. Use the largest squares, 1" x 1" units, for the main focus, then use the smaller squares and triangles as the supporting elements (or you can use the 1/2" x 1" rectangle to make half a block).

The procedure for designing set arrangements is the same as designing blocks except that the design elements are restricted. Study Figure 2-19 to see an example of a block that can be used as a set arrangement. The dark squares represent the location of a pieced or appliqué block.

The trick to converting the block design into a setting arrangement is changing the scale when you cut templates. Normally, on the grid pages you've been using, you would translate 1/4" on the grid page to 1" on the actual quilt. In the set arrangements, the ratio becomes 1/4" equals 3". If Figure 2-19 was a block, it would be 10" x 12". As a set arrangement, the size would be 30" x 36".

Designing unique set arrangements is very liberating with this method. You move around the large squares until you have a pleasing set. You fill in the larger background areas with smaller geometric units. The result is a new set arrangement.

Note: In these first arrangements, I used very simple geometric units as the filler elements. As you work with this technique, you will probably select filler units that relate in some way to the block or blocks you have chosen. Select some unit from the block and perhaps reduce it in size and use it as fill. This coordinates the entire design.

Figure 2-20 shows another possible set arrangement. Remember that the long rectangle spaces hold half a block. Not all your blocks can be divided in half to work in this way. If your design can't be divided, you shouldn't use the large rectangles as design elements.

Figure 2-19

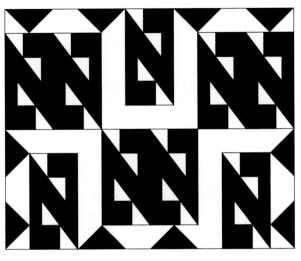

Wall quilt size 30" x 36".
This represents the use of the design technique to cre-
ate quilt block settings. A piecework block of your
choice would be placed in the large black square
areas. Half a block could be placed in the large rec-
tangular areas.

Wall quilt set with blocks in place 30" x 36".

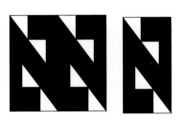

The piecework
block from Figure
1-7 is placed in the
set arrangement. A
half block was
substituted for the
large rectangles.

Figure 2-20

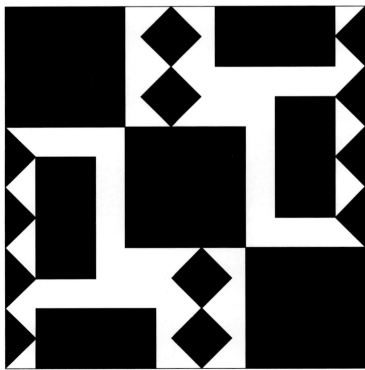

A set arrangement with 12" blocks and half blocks. The quilt
size is 36" x 36".

Creative Idea -
From Block to Vest

I enjoy making vests for myself and for sale, so I am always looking for new and interesting designs for the fronts of my vests. I discovered that some of the quilt blocks I design could be modified to make them suitable as vest fronts. Here is the procedure I use.

Step 1. Measure your vest to determine its length and width. Add 2" to each measurement, then add whatever you need to arrive at even numbers. This is the size block you need to create. In my case, I needed a block 14" x 26".

Step 2. Look through the library of block designs you have created. Select one that is asymmetrical and try working with that. I selected Block #5 and adapted it to create a rectangular block in the size I needed. In the original block, 1/4" equaled 1" when translated to the size of the templates. Thus, the original block was 10" x 10". In doing the adaptation, I made 1/4" equal 2". My block then became 20" x 20". I then cut some units

from the side of the block, added units to the bottom, and shifted interior units until I created a block that looked pleasing in the size I required. I needed a block approximately 14" x 26" (see Figure 2-21).

Step 3. Select fabric colors, cut out the pieces, and sew the block together. You can then cut the vest front from this fabric block.

Step 4. To create the other side of the vest, you can use the same block turned upside-down so the two sides don't look the same. Or you can strip piece the other side of the vest, repeating the use of the fabrics from the block side. See my vest on page 32 .

You have now learned how to work with the blocks you create. You have discovered how the development of a single block can lead to a design for an entire quilt. I have worked with smaller wall-size quilts in these exercises, but to create a full-size quilt you simply multiply the number of blocks in your design.

The next chapter will show you another way to create a wall quilt using a medallion format rather than a block format. Take out your design elements, turn the page, and let's have some more fun!

Figure 2-21

Original Block #5 10" x 10"

Block used for vest fronts. Turn the block upside-down for the right front. The block size needed for my vest was 14" x 26", but this will vary depending on the size vest you are making.

Baltimore by Machine (27" x 22"). Designed, sewn, and hand-quilted by Joyce Mori. Large design element pieces were moved around on the grid paper to form the setting. I added the blue sashing to separate the elements. I used some of the wonderful floral motifs on the design cards for my Pfaff 7570. They looked like Baltimore album quilt designs so I put them into this setting to have my own machine-made Baltimore.

Vest from a Quilt Design. Designed and sewn by Joyce Mori. The asymmetric vest fronts are created by designing a large quilt block and then cutting the fronts from it. Blue denim is combined with machine embroidered flower motifs and bright red flower prints.

Geometrics (32" x 36"). Designed, sewn, and hand-quilted by Joyce Mori. Square and rectangular design elements were used to create a modern block and four blocks were combined to form the quilt. The center square in each block is constructed crazy patch fabric. Wild colors plus the black and white stripe make this a wild, contemporary-looking quilt.

Elegance (18¾" x 19¾"). Designed, sewn, hand- and machine-quilted by Joyce Mori. The large square and rectangle design elements were used to devise a quilt setting. The square and rectangular blocks were then filled with machine-embroidered designs using a Pfaff 7570 and design cards.

Wild Primitive Designs (23½" x 23½"). Designed and hand-quilted by Joyce Mori. The quilt set was created using larger geometric square and rectangle design elements. I filled the larger units with machine embroidery done with design cards and my Pfaff 7570.

Which Design to Feature? (32" x 32"). Designed, sewn, and hand-quilted by Joyce Mori. This is Block #52. This design has many wonderful possibilities for coloration. There are hidden stars and pinwheels in the quilt. How you color the design determines which features will be emphasized.

Chapter 3

Medallion Style Wall Quilts

esigning wall quilts in the medallion style means there will be a main central unit surrounded by smaller units. Take a momentary breather from your designing, then pick up your scissors and sheets of card stock elements and cut out the larger motifs.

Choose a few of your favorite larger units and make sure you have two copies of each. When designing larger projects instead of blocks, you'll need to cut out additional pieces of the basic units. The larger the project you design, the more elements you will need to fill in space. So whenever you have a few moments, cut out additional design elements, but don't yet cut out the diagonal elements. Store all the design elements in a plastic storage container or zip lock bag so they won't get lost.

Spray a grid graph page with spray adhesive (see the Helpful Hint on page 11). Keep a few extra paper copies of the grid graph page beside you. Place the large design elements and some of the basic smaller elements in front of you. Choose a large unit and place it at the approximate center on the grid graph page. Add another unit to this, perhaps its mirror image.

Study how it looks. If you like it, glue the paper versions of the elements on a paper page and set this page aside. Repeat the design process with some of the other large units.

These examples illustrate three medallion center options. Figure 3-1 is an enclosed rectangle, Figure 3-2 is a cross shape with naturally occurring open areas between the arms of the cross, and Figure 3-3 shows a shape with many open areas between the separate elements. Each of these alternatives makes a workable medallion center.

After you've created several combinations, select one you like and place its elements back down on the adhesive page. This is the unit you will use as you work through the ideas in this chapter.

Figure 3-1

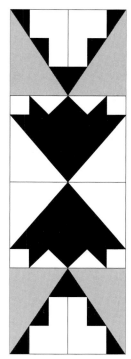

A rectangular medallion unit.

Figure 3-2

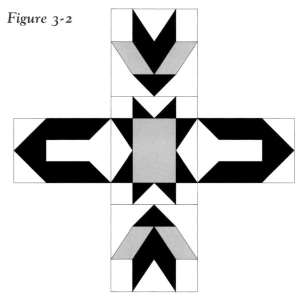

A center medallion in a cross shape. The spaces between the arms of the cross can be filled in with extra units.

Figure 3-3

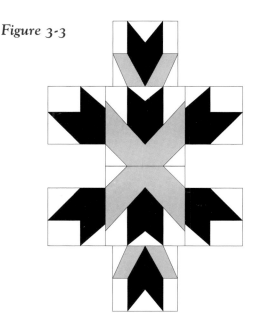

This is a more complex central medallion.

Helpful Hint

It may be necessary to tape four copies of the grid graph page together to form a large sheet. You could also buy a large sheet of four-squares-to-the-inch graph paper at an office supply store. When you begin to design medallion style quilts or any large size quilt, you will need a larger surface on which to place your design elements as you create the quilt. Using a single grid graph page allows you to create a wall quilt that is approximately 32" by 36".

Now that you have created a central focus unit—a medallion—you need to expand its size. The process is very simple. You merely add new elements to the central medallion area until you fill in the blank areas of the grid graph page. In

Figure 3-5

A larger medallion design built up from the design in Figure 3-2. The star unit is placed in the open areas.

Figure 3-4

Extra elements are added to the starting medallion from Figure 3-1 to create the center focus area of a wall quilt.

Figure 3-6

The center medallion has its open areas filled in and a series of framing elements are added to the design.

some cases, your starting medallion may be so large it almost fills the grid graph page so you won't have to add many other elements. Figures 3-4, 3-5, and 3-6 show how I took each of the three medallion units and filled in the open areas to create a wall quilt design.

How do you decide which elements to use? An analysis of the illustrations will give you some ideas.

- ❀ Repeat separate elements from the medallion or use mirror images of the elements.
- ❀ Select other units that match up along one side.
- ❀ Select some elements that can act as enclosing units to contain or frame a design.
- ❀ Select units that in some way reinforce the shapes of the main medallion.

When you complete designs you like, glue the paper elements of the design on a grid graph sheet and make four copies as you did when you were designing blocks.

If you want to make a larger wall quilt or even a bed quilt with your newly created design, tape four copies of the medallion quilt together to make a larger quilt. Add medallion sections together until you have the size you want (Figures 3-7 and 3-8).

There is a second way to create a central medallion unit to be the basis for your wall quilt design. Use four-block, nine-block, or 16-block combinations as the central medallion. The multiple block center unit becomes a replacement for a design built of the larger size elements. Figures 3-9 and 3-10 take you through the steps of this designing strategy.

Figure 3-7

Four units from Figure 3-4 placed together to create a larger size quilt.

Figure 3-8

Nine medallion units of Figure 3-6 placed together. Notice how the framing elements form a sashing for the quilt. This is a really exciting design.

This central unit (medallion) consists of 12 blocks put together in a cross-like formation. The original block is very simple, just two triangle elements combined. There is a wonderful pinwheel design at the center of the design. I designed a number of interesting central medallion designs from this triangle element and its mirror image. I hope you will work with this unit also.

Using the 12-block medallion design, add four blocks in the empty corner spaces. The blocks in the corners are larger than the corner space, so add plain filler rectangles. Turn over a black element and use its reverse side (white) to create a filler unit or allow the grid graph background to show, thus representing additional background area.

The block still sticks out from the main design, so add long elements to connect the corners to each other. These units frame the entire design. I like the framing portion of this design so much that I'm going to try it on other medallion units.

Figure 3-11 shows another example of a central medallion created from blocks. This design uses a four-block unit from Figure 1-7 repeated four times to form a design. There's a lot of dark space in this design that could be used as a background area for appliqué designs or could be divided into additional units.

The last set of examples in this chapter illustrates a final way to build out from medallion center units. Find the card stock page of diagonal units in your folder and cut out some of the units. These diagonal units provide immediate directional focus for your central medallion. They are intended to be placed in any of the designs that have open corner areas such as the cross forms. I inserted diagonal units in the corners of the center medallion of Figure 3-2 to create the wonderful quilt design in Figure 3-12. I added another element to the ends of the diagonal units to finish them off, to keep the diagonal from appearing to go off the edge of the paper.

Notice that four designs have been placed together and a new design is formed at the center point where the four medallion units meet. You might want to use the center design as a jumping off point for creating a new design. Designing also

Figure 3-9

A single block is formed.

A central medallion unit composed of 12 blocks. A wonderful double pinwheel is formed.

Figure 3-10

A framing pattern is added to the central medallion to create a wall quilt design.

involves taking advantage of the serendipitous combinations that occur when units are combined.

In Figure 3-13, a very simple diagonal element was added to each corner. I used only one part of the three-part element in each corner. When four of the medallions are combined, new designs are formed at each outer edge and the center.

Try adding diagonal units to your designs to see how they look. You may have to cut off or add onto a diagonal unit to make it fit in the open space. Diagonals don't work on every design, but they are one of your designing options.

Figure 3-11

A four-block unit from Figure 1-7 is repeated four times to create a center medallion.

The medallion with corner diagonal units.

Figure 3-13

Four medallions have been combined. A new center pinwheel is formed.

Figure 3-12

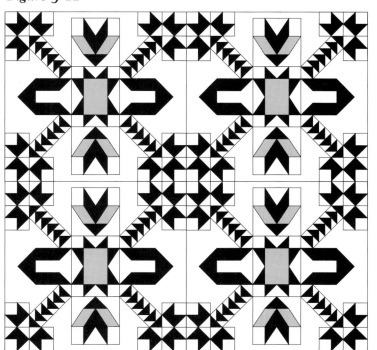

The combination of four medallion units from Figure 3-2 with diagonal elements in the corners produce this exciting design.

One of the best ways to really explore the possibilities of a combination of elements, a block, or an entire medallion design is to work in a series. This means trying many combinations and many strategies to modify a single design (see Chapter 4). I suggest you keep a copy of all the designs you develop, even those that don't meet your needs at the time. As you become more familiar with the design process, you may be able to modify a design to produce an even more exciting result.

Kaleidoscope
(24" x 24").
Designed, sewn, and
hand-quilted by Joyce
Mori. The center of
the design features a
long, right angle
triangle and its mirror
image. The design was
colored to create the
expanding star from
these units. The back-
ground was divided
into light and medium
turquoise areas to add
more interest to the
quilt.

Fall Color (30" x 30").
Designed, sewn, and
hand-quilted by Joyce
Mori. Block #40 was
repeated four times
for the main area of the
quilt. The border repeats
a triangle element from
the main block.

Diamonds (31" x 36"). Designed, sewn, and hand-quilted by Joyce Mori.
This is an example of a wall quilt designed from repeated elements.
Some of the diamond shapes were emphasized by using darker fabrics.

Chapter 4

Modifications to Blocks and Quilt Designs

I don't want to put a damper on your designing efforts, but it's likely that not all your designs have turned out to your satisfaction. However, I hope you've kept them all in a folder for future use. Now is the time to bring out the less than perfect designs. Artists recognize that it's important to know when to stop working on a painting. They must prevent themselves from overworking a picture. The same thing can be said of designing. You have to know when to quit adding elements so you don't end up with a cluttered design, but it's also true that there is often room for improvement. Now you are going to look at your previously rejected designs in terms of how you might change and hopefully improve them.

Modifications can be made on both block and quilt designs. Just remember that not all ideas work with all blocks or quilts and not all changes improve a design. You are trying creative options.

Option #1 - Filling in with Extra Units

You already know that one design strategy is to simplify a block by reducing the number of design elements in it. Study Block #9, which is a very open block. Below is an illustration that shows four of these simple blocks placed together. Additional illustrations on this page show two versions of the block with additional elements added to it. When four of these new blocks are put together, totally different designs result. And these designs can easily be further modified.

Modified block

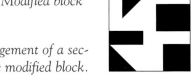

A four-block arrangement of a second version of the modified block. A large center square appears and a pinwheel design can be seen in the negative space.

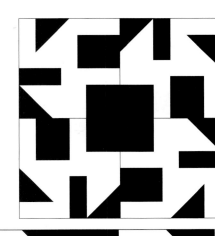

Figure 4-1

Block #9

A four-block arrangement of the original block.

A four-block arrangement of the modified block. There is a definite line in the design and a zigzag motif can be seen.

Modified block

The modifications to Anastasia Pavlovic's block (Figure 4-2) result in a truly different quilt design. In the original block, the open space of the block allows the pinwheel motifs, formed when blocks were rotated 90 degrees and combined, to be isolated. The quilt has a light, open appearance. Despite the very geometric nature of the design, the quilt would be lovely done in pastel, reproduction prints.

When the block is modified by placing units in the center of the block, all the elements touch. The quilt design in Figure 4-2 shows 16 of the new blocks combined. This design has no open space to feature individual units. However, vertical and horizontal lines can be seen. There are a number of ways to color this design to emphasize the vertical, horizontal, and diagonal interest of the quilt.

Figure 4-3 shows one of Pat Hill's blocks with modifications. Notice that when the additional elements are added to the block, the diagonal design is less prominent. The diagonal units are competing for attention with the large squares and small triangles. Obviously, the way you put the blocks together also affects the appearance of the design.

Figure 4-2

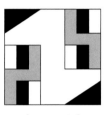

Anastasia's
original Block
#36AP

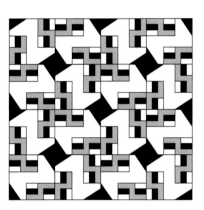

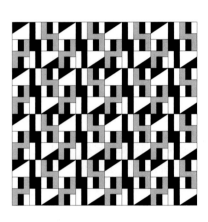

Modified block
with additional
elements added.

Figure 4-3

Pat's original
Block #27PH

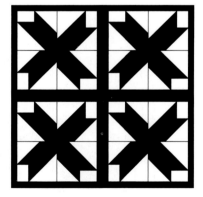

These diagrams show two wall quilt variations when 16 blocks are combined.

Modified block
with additional
elements added

This design contains 16 of the same modified block. It features the same layout as the top left design in Figure 4-3.

Option #2 - Subtracting Elements

A block can also be modified by subtracting elements, usually revealing more background space. Figure 4-4 shows one of Anastasia Pavlovic's blocks that has been modified by deleting some elements. This creates an area of light background that frames a square on two sides. This square could feature a small appliqué motif, a machine-embroidered design, or a specific fabric.

The general principle of modifying a block by adding or subtracting units also applies to your quilt designs or your combinations of blocks. If a design appears too confusing, subtract some elements or parts of elements and create more background.

Figure 4-4

Nine blocks are combined to form this wall quilt. The squares could be used to feature a small applique design or a lovely special fabric.

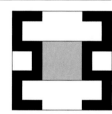

Block #35AP Anastasia's modified block with one element removed

Figure 4-5

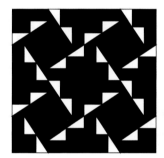

Original four-block design

The design is altered by the subtraction of some units.

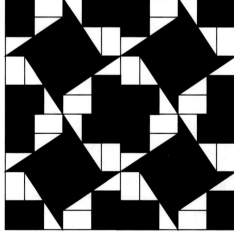

The addition of color to the various elements in the design opens up the design without subtracting more elements.

Helpful Hint

An easy way to see how a design will look with more visible white space is to cover areas of the elements with pieces of white card stock. You can do this by using the reverse side of your elements, frequently the squares and rectangles. This allows you to blot out part of the black space without having to cut away part of the design or painting it with correction fluid.

Just as you can have too little background, you can also have too much. In this case, you will need to add some elements to create a design with more definition.

Figure 4-6

Pat Hill's original Block #29PH

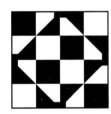

Four of the original blocks combined

This 16-block combination appears static.

Additional squares are added to some of the blocks in this design after 16 of the original blocks are combined.

Don't be discouraged when a design appears to contain too much dark space. Remember you are designing in black and white. Eventually, you will convert these designs to color; frequently the problem disappears as you add color/values to your project (see Figure 4-5).

Option #3 - Substituting Elements

Substitution is a very easy way to change the appearance of a block. In fact, with this technique you will probably change the dimensions of the block also, depending on the number of shapes you substitute. The concept is very simple. If you have a square shape in the block, substitute a rectangle. If you have an equal-sided right triangle, substitute one with unequal sides. Likewise, you can exchange one size rectangle for another size, either larger or smaller. Designing with templates makes it easy to make these changes without any drawing required. You can quickly change sizes by changing the templates on the grid graph or grid block pages, then decide if the change is desirable (see Figures 4-7 and 4-8).

Option #4 - Cutting Elements Apart

You don't have to work with the elements exactly as they appear in this book. Many elements can be easily modified in some way, perhaps by cutting them apart and putting them together with another element, with more space between the parts, or with fewer parts. With this technique, you are really creating new elements. And of course, new elements lead to new designs.

Here's an example of this principle using just one element. I created a four-block unit with the element and then combined four of those blocks to create a center medallion (see Figure 3-11). However, when I looked at the design I felt it was too overpowering because of the amount of black in the design. The quilt needed to be lightened up,

Figure 4-7

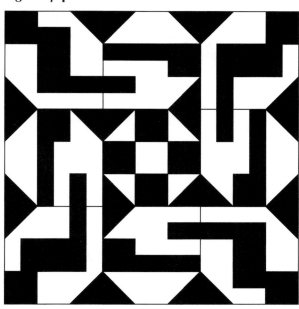

This design is a modification of Figure 2-10. Study both figures and decide if you think the changes improve the design. I substituted elements to reduce the blockiness or heaviness I felt appeared when the blocks were combined.

Figure 4-8

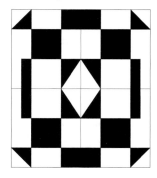 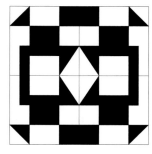

This is a modification of Block #2 from Chapter 1. Notice the four-block design. A mirror image of the block is also used.

This is another modification of Block #2 from Chapter 1. Notice the four-block combination. A mirror image of the block is also used.

Figure 4-9

This is the original element

These three illustrations show versions of the element as it is modified by removing part of the element. The new element is combined four times to create a block. Four of the four-block designs are combined to create each of these wall quilt designs. Each is truly unique.

 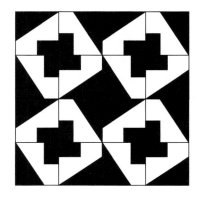 

so I modified the original element and repeated the entire design process and created three new quilt designs (see Figure 4-9).

I think my new designs are much improved and present a more dynamic appearance, and I have some new elements to use in future design work. As you create new elements, you can glue them on a piece of paper and copy them on card stock. They can then be used in the same way as the elements in this book.

Keep your eyes open for new design elements. Study floor tiles, decorator fabrics, modern art, etc. Whenever you see a new combination of geometric units, sketch it. As you have time, draw these new elements on graph paper or in your computer drawing program. Use them to design as you use the elements provided with this book.

Most of the elements in this book were drawn with ease of cutting and sewing in mind. As you become familiar with my design ideas, you may want to draw very unusual design elements which require individual templates to cut them out. Using such design elements allows you to create very unique quilt and block designs.

Figure 4-10

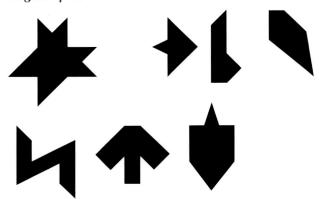

These elements have very unusual shapes. Overlay them with the plastic grid sheet to see how they can be broken down into basic geometric shapes. In many cases, when you use such elements you will need to draw templates to cut them out.

Helpful Hint

If you have a computer drawing program, you can draw new elements and print that page on regular paper, then copy it on card stock. Or you can print directly to card stock if your printer will accept the thicker paper.

When you apply the modification strategies, you are really working on a design, block, or quilt in a series. This technique is widely used by quilt designers to explore the potential of a design they have created. They add, subtract, or alter their designs in some way to find the potential range a design has for visual impact through vertical, horizontal, or diagonal lines or through focus on a motif. You don't always have to start from scratch in the design process—you can alter a design to create something new. In fact, the modification process may stretch your creative designing talents to a greater degree than creating an entirely new design.

The modification process helps you better understand what makes a successful design. What changes did you make to improve it? What changes were unsatisfactory? You will probably want to try modifying even your terrific designs. After working in a series to modify a design, your understanding of the design process will become clearer. Does asymmetry work better than symmetry? Are triangles in corners effective design choices? Should elements touch or be spaced apart? As with any task in life, the more you practice, the more you learn and improve. If only I had realized that when I tried to avoid practicing the piano!

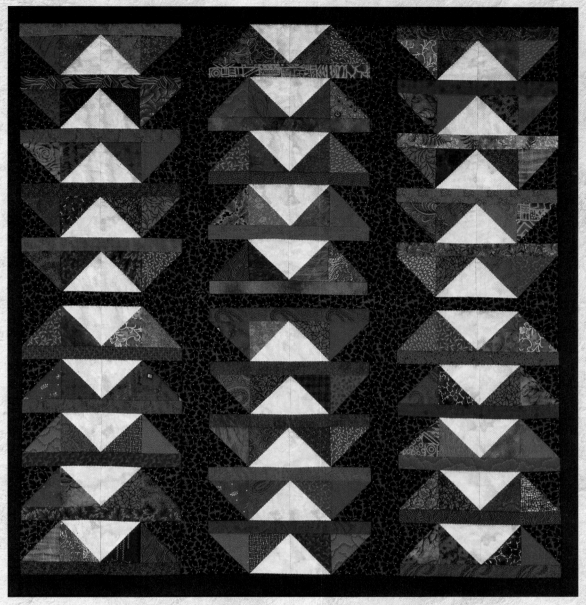

Colorful Scraps (42½" x 44"). Designed, sewn, and hand-quilted by Joyce Mori. Block #58 is the basis for the quilt. The black print sets off the bright red, blue, purple, and green scrap triangles.

(8" x 8"). Block #41.
The neutral coloring of this block
gives it a contemporary feel.

(12" x 12"). Block #53.
Bright hand-dyed fabrics are used against
a white background to create a block with
a joyful, happy look.

Wow! (51" x 39"). Designed, sewn, and machine-quilted by Joyce Mori. Four designing elements were used to make each block. In some blocks they were turned inward and in others outward. A lovely hand-painted green fabric forms the background.

(11" x 16"). Block #42. There are many possibilities for coloring this block. The red squares form a diagonal line which could be reinforced in a multiple-block arrangement.

Contemporary (37½″ x 37½″). Designed and sewn by
Joyce Mori. Hand-quilted by Barbara Pavlovic and
Joyce Mori. This quilt features Block #36AP created by
Anastasia Pavlovic, age nine. Fabrics were supplied by
RJR fabrics and include Basic Realities, Quilt Back
prints, and Marble Montage collections.

Block #4 (24″ x 24″). The separate square and
rectangular elements in this block were cut from
strip-pieced dyed fabric. The neutral gray background
allowed the strip pieced units to visually stand out. The
scale of the block was changed to 1/4″ equals 2″. This
enlarged the single block to the size of a small wall quilt.

Pinwheels and Stars (23½" x 23½"). Designed, sewn, and hand-quilted by Joyce Mori.
Block #56 was used for this quilt. The border was formed by adding additional elements in the block.
A decorative machine maxi stitch on my Pfaff 7570 was used to add interest to the blue rectangles of
the pinwheel. Don't ignore all the wonderful features of today's computerized sewing machines.

Borders

fter trying the techniques in the previous chapters, you will have created some lovely wall quilt or quilt designs, or at least the central portion of such designs. Now it's time to consider borders.

Why do you want to add borders to a quilt design? Flip back to Chapter 2 and look at some of the multiple-block designs. They look unfinished. The designs don't seem to have a stopping point, they just run off the edge of the paper. A border stops the design. It can make a quilt look finished. It surrounds the design and encloses it. Visually, there is a final resolution to the design.

Each quilt design dictates its own border treatment. Some designs require very simple borders, perhaps only a strip of fabric on all edges. Other designs may require something more elaborate. Sometimes a design can have both simple and elaborate borders. A plain strip of fabric might be the first border and a pieced border or border with appliqué might be the second one. There may be a final border that is only a plain strip of fabric. A quilt can have more than one border.

Some blocks or designs may come with built-in borders. Look at the top right illustration in Figure 4-3 and notice how the rectangular element on the two sides of the block produces a simple border when 16 blocks are combined. You could choose to leave the design as is or you might add another "true" border to this quilt.

The width of your border must be kept in proper proportion to the size of the quilt. There is no magic formula for this, but an 8" border on a central design made of 16 6" blocks would probably be out of place. I usually try to make the border one third or one fourth the measurement of the block. If I am using a 12" block, the border width might be 3" or 4". This gives me a starting point from which to modify the width if necessary. The larger the total size of the project,

the wider the border can be. A wall quilt of 6" blocks should probably have a narrower border than a full size quilt of 6" blocks. But design considerations and personal preference will also influence the width of the border.

Pull out your quilt designs and design elements and let's explore some options for designing borders.

Option #1 - Extending Lines or Adding to Units

With some designs, it's possible to simply extend some lines of the design into the border area. This serves to complete or finish off a design. Figure 5-1 shows how easily this can work. Only 12 small lines were added to the quilt to provide an easy finish to the design. These lines formed eight triangles. When I penciled in extended lines where

Figure 5-1

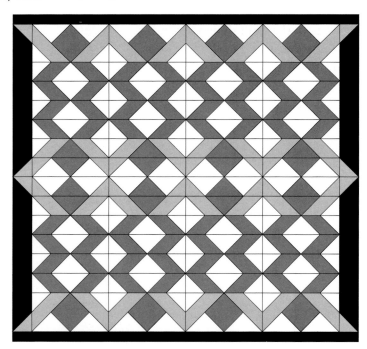

The lines of some of the outside units are extended and triangles are formed. These triangles appear to complete the design. Dark side borders are added to set off the triangles. Strip borders are added to the top and bottom to balance the design.

they appeared cut-off on the design, I quickly noticed that triangles were being formed and I liked the result. I used some of my cutout elements set down in the proper location on the design to easily visualize how this would look. Then I added narrow strips to the top and bottom of the design to provide a visual balance. My borders were complete.

With this technique, I worked with a pencil on a paper copy of the design before selecting the actual elements to fit in place on the illustration. After the triangles were glued in place, I made a copy of the completed design.

Option #2 - Repeating Units

With this option, you simply repeat one or more of the elements from the main design in the border areas. This technique can visually unify a design and serves to maintain harmony in the design by not adding unrelated geometric forms.

Begin by moving the original elements in the quilt design around in the border area to see if any of them will work to create a border design.

Figure 5-2 shows how this can be easily done. Notice that the square with the center rectangle was repeated. In the corners, the triangle was repeated and a narrow rectangle was repeated to form part of a narrow border. As you look at this design, you see that the borders have brought more emphasis and attention to the dark rectangles surrounded by the light strips on all sides.

Figure 5-2

Notice the repeat of the triangles in the corners, the rectangles extending outward, and the narrow rectangles along the outside edge. A sewn example of this design is shown below.

Intersections (32" x 32"). Designed, sewn, and hand-quilted by Joyce Mori. Block #14 was repeated four times to create the quilt. The border repeats some of the units of the block.

Option #3 - Selecting New Units

You've probably noticed that some designing elements are long and narrow. These units can often be used in the border. You can also create your own long and narrow units by putting smaller units together to use in a border. Figure 5-3 shows examples of long units.

Select some long units and move them around on the outside of your design. When you determine that one works well in the design, use the multiple copies to actually create a border. Consider leaving a narrow space, to be sewn as a strip of fabric, as an inner border to separate the main body of the quilt from the border. This technique frames and emphasizes the central design even more. Decide if this inner border should be kept white or made dark.

You will probably find that the units don't always magically fit along the border space. Several strategies can be used to fit the borders. Try separating out the units by putting one at each end of a side, then decide if any more units can be added in the middle. If an entire unit won't fit in the center,

perhaps you can fill in an empty space with a square or rectangle. I used a square fill in the quilt design shown in Figure 5-4.

You might also try placing the selected border units at the center of a quilt side and working outward from that point. Your areas of fill, if needed, will be in the corners. You might be able to fill in a corner with a basic geometric element or you might be able to draw connecting lines to create a unified corner. In Figure 5-5, a small rectangle fill was needed before the corner area could be completed.

Another strategy is to use more than one long element in the border. A combination of two or three units might create a border that fits the space. Border elements don't have to butt up against each other. Consider leaving empty space between the elements—a rectangle or square—to achieve a border design. You can also cut apart the individual units of a border element and place them in the border area with white space separating them.

Working with elements for the border is a trial and error process. Just take your time and try many different options before making your final decision. This designing process allows you to quickly consider many possibilities.

Figure 5-3

Long narrow units.

Two units combined.

Figure 5-4

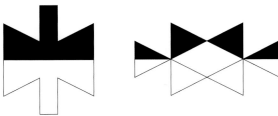 *The border unit I selected.*

Notice that additional triangles are formed when the units are combined. On the long sides, the units don't fit evenly, so a fill square is added at the center. A triangle is added in each corner to tie the borders together. A narrow inner border is attached to the sides of the quilt design and it serves to separate the quilt design from the borders, creating two distinct parts.

Figure 5-5

The border elements are placed at the center and moved outward on this design using Block #16. This leaves a short space near each corner where a border unit won't fit. Three triangles and two rectangular fills are used as corner fill to complete the design.

Figure 5-6

The dark areas represent the possible new border units.

Create a Quilt

Figure 5-7

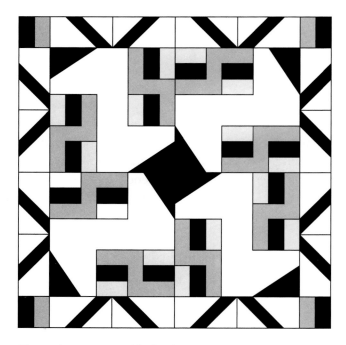

Original unit. The dark area indicates the section cut off and used in the border.

Four of Anastasia's blocks (see page 44) combined and a border of a cutoff unit added.

The element is cut in half and a triangle is also cut out and used.

The center medallion is Block #28PH (see page 101) that is doubled in size. The border consists of a series of cutoff elements.

Option #4 - Using Parts of Elements

To make border elements fit a space or to create a new border element, consider cutting apart sections of elements to make them fit. Study all the design elements and decide if you could make border units from them by cutting them in half to create new long, narrow design elements. Figure 5-6 shows examples of how cutting apart design elements can form new elements for border designs.

Just as you did for Option #3, place these elements around the outside of your quilt design to see how they might work into a border. Figure 5-7 shows some "new" border elements placed around the edges of two quilt designs.

Option #5- Isolating Elements

Normally, you might think of a border design as consisting of a continuous set of elements or a continuous strip enclosing and encircling the outside edge of the design. However, some borders

consist of elements separated from one another and spaced evenly around the outside of the design. This is somewhat akin to placing small quilt blocks around the edges of a quilt. Figure 5-8 shows an example of a quilt with such a design strategy.

Obviously, the more complex a design and its borders become, the longer it will take to sew. Sewing time might be a consideration if you are making a quilt project as a gift or have a limited amount of time to complete it. However, a more detailed design often has tremendous visual impact. You must strike a balance between your time constraints and the detail you put into a design. If you create a lovely, complex design that you don't have time to sew, place the design in a folder for future consideration. I have a folder of projects labeled "Retirement Projects."

Option #6- Using Different Borders on Each Side

There is no rule that says the borders on all four sides of a quilt must be the same. Perhaps you would like complex borders on two sides and simple borders on the other two sides. Using different border design strategy options may give you one set of borders on the top and bottom and a different set of borders on the sides. In Figure 5-9, two examples are illustrated.

It may be that you need wider borders on two sides and narrower borders on the other sides to achieve a specific size quilt or project.

Mixed borders are a variation of Option #6. Divide the border area in half or in thirds.

A tiny block and its mirror image are spaced along the sides of the quilt to form a border in this design using Block #17. The rectangles at the corners tie each border together.

Figure 5-8

Tiny block

Make one part pieced and the remainder plain. You can place the pieced section in any part of the border. In Figure 5-10, the pieced sections were placed in the corners.

The border is the last part of the quilt you design. This doesn't mean it shouldn't be given considerable thought and attention. If you get stuck on how to treat a border, look at pictures of Navajo or Persian rugs and study picture books of award-winning quilts. Arrive at some general ideas of how weavers and other quilters handle borders and see if you can adapt any of those strategies to your designs.

You may decide you don't want an actual border added to your quilt design. You can still frame the design area by adding a dark binding to the quilt. Even though the binding is narrow, the dark value of this narrow strip will enclose the design area.

Figure 5-9

This quilt project has six blocks as the center. The top and bottom borders are different from the two side borders.

Block #18

This quilt has a center design area and different borders on the sides and top and bottom.

Figure 5-10

This shows an example of mixed borders with the pieced sections in the corners.

Pinwheels and Squares (26″ x 26″).
Designed by Joyce Mori from Block #26PH created by Pat Hill of West Hills, Calif.
The quilt was sewn and machine-quilted by Pat.
Fabrics in the quilt are from the RJR Basic Realities collection.

Triangles Everywhere (44" x 44"). The quilt was designed by Joyce Mori using Block #30PH created by Pat Hill. The quilt was sewn and machine-quilted by Pat. The quilt features a wonderful blue/orange color scheme in several values of the colors. Horizontal rows of light and dark orange squares can be seen in this quilt. Fabrics are from the RJR Basic Realities collection.

Bright and Colorful (41" x 50"). Designed and sewn by Joyce Mori. Hand-quilted by Delores Stemple of Aurora, West Virginia. Eight #24 blocks were used for the quilt, with two turned horizontally in the center of the quilt. The border features a repeat of one unit in the block separated by a square.

Summer Flowers (31½" x 31½"). Design is by Theresa Fleming, Aurora, Colo. The quilt was sewn and hand-quilted by Joyce Mori. The flower blocks are Block #32TF. Lovely pastel 1930 era reproduction prints give the quilt a bright, summery look.

Chapter 6

Color Shading a Design

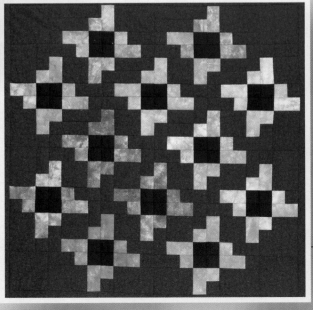

hus far, the design elements you've been working with have been rendered in black and white with an occasional bit of gray shading added. This is to show the distinct contrast between the colors. When you study a design in black and white, your eyes focus on the elements, the patterns created, the points of emphasis, etc. There is no distraction from the introduction of colors and their shadings. If a design has no visual interest in black and white, it probably won't have any pizzazz in other colors.

Before I discuss color ideas, there is one more option to consider in the black and white format—reversing the white and black areas. A block or design can look quite different when the black and white areas are reversed. This is not to say that both arrangements are equally as successful but that you should consider the option. Interesting designs can result. Reversing the positive/negative (black/white) shadings emphasizes different sections of a design (see Figure 6-1).

In a design that uses white, gray, and black for the shading, you'll see new designs when the three shadings are reversed. There are more ways to switch three shadings around than two (see Figure 6-2). Only one shading option is shown, but you can easily work with this design and create other options.

The examples shown illustrate that completely different designs emerge when you reverse the black/white areas. As you study designs, consider reversing the black/white shading before adding color. It's important to play with as many of the options available to you before you finalize the design for sewing.

There are no only-gray-shaded elements in the design element sheets in this book, but in the Appendix you'll find pages of line drawings of elements with no fill added. You can work with these elements using the options in this text to enable you to easily reverse black/white shadings or add gray shadings.

Figure 6-1

A grouping of four blocks. The original block is on page 100 in the Appendix.

The black/white shading is reversed and a four-block grouping is made with the new shading.

Figure 6-2

A grouping of four blocks. The original block is located on page 99 in the Appendix.

A grouping of the same block with the shading reversed.

Helpful Hint

If you are using a computer drawing program, you can use it to change the fill areas. Likewise, you can easily create a line drawing of the project by removing all the fill. This allows you to color in the design on your computer or to print out the design and color it with pens or pencils.

Option #1

Put the design together with unshaded elements. This saves drawing the design on graph paper. You have a design that can be colored or shaded in as you desire. Make several copies of this drawing before you begin to change the shading or add color. With a permanent black marker, ink in the new areas you want to make black and leave the other areas of the element white. You can later use another copy of this unshaded line drawing and color in the appropriate areas with colored pencils or markers to create your color scheme.

Figure 6-3 shows an example of a line drawing. Notice that seeing a design with only lines offers you additional opportunities to find areas to shade or delineate. You may even make additional modifications to the design when you see it as a line drawing.

Option #2

Color some of the line drawing elements gray and replace some black or white areas of your design with the gray elements. This helps you visualize how you can separate out other areas of the design. Using the gray elements helps you isolate other areas of interest in a block or quilt. You have essentially three ways to delineate a design—with white, gray, or black elements. You have the advantage of being able to isolate sections without the distraction of actual colors (see Figure 6-4).

Spend some time studying the design you've created. Tack the design to a wall and stand back. Can areas of the design be separated out from each other? Is there movement or line in the design that can be emphasized? As you study the design and understand the nature of the design, you can select

Figure 6-3

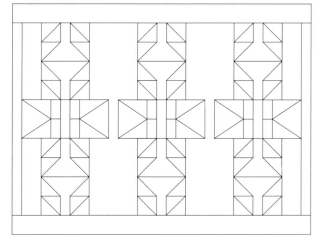

This is a line drawing of a design with all shading removed.

Figure 6-4

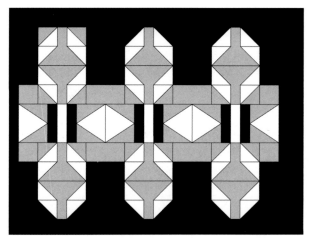

Shading is added and the design is modified from the original line drawing. Once the shading is in place, you begin to see areas of the design develop.

and isolate areas of the design that can be eventually rendered in different colors.

The Color Scheme

Once you've created an exciting and interesting design, it's time to consider color options. There are many interesting and effective books on the market to aid you in selecting colors for your quilt. I'm not going to deal with the intricacies of color theory in this book. I highly recommend that you buy an artist's color wheel to help you understand and develop a color scheme. This wheel is not used to select actual colors, but to help you understand color strategies.

Option #1 - Using Artist's Pre-Selected Color Palettes

The following books will provide instruction for selecting color combinations: *Color Harmony 2* by Bride M. Whelan, *Living Colors* by Margaret Walch and Augustine Hope, *Designer's Guide to Color* by Chronicle Books (there are five books in

the series), *The Patchwork Pocket Palette* by Anne Walker, *Color Magic for Quilters* by Ann Seely and Joyce Stewart, and *Color for Quilters* (small booklet) by Lauri Linch-Zadel.

These books show example after example of color combinations. The combinations are based on art principles, but it isn't really necessary for you to understand those principles at the beginning. All you really need to know is that there are certain color harmonies or combinations that can provide the jumping off point when selecting colors for your quilt. When you utilize these books, you take advantage of the fact that someone else has already selected colors that can work together. This strategy is perfect when you really don't know what color combinations you want to use. Mark the pages of combinations that really appeal to you, color in your drawing with those colors, then go to your favorite fabric store and select fabrics that represent those combinations.

The translation from colored pencil to fabric is not automatic. Groupings of fabrics influence how each looks with the other. But the pre-selected color palette can be a basis for your selection of actual fabrics.

Option #2 - The Color Wheel

You can also use a color wheel to select colors and help you understand why a particular set of colors work together. Color wheels have the various color strategies built into them. For instance, if you want a quilt with green in it, you need to know what other colors might work well in it. By selecting green as the key color on the color wheel, you'll see the colors that are analogous to green—yellow, yellow green, blue green, and blue. Thus an analogous scheme would be one combination possibility.

The color wheel also shows that the direct complement to green is red and so this combination or harmony is possible. Two other interesting harmonies are green with orange and violet (triadic) and green with red orange and red violet (split complement). The color wheel automatically selects, so to speak, the combination option for you to look at.

I find that starting with one color I really like is a wonderful way to explore the possible harmonies I can use with that color. Many of the combinations aren't ones I would normally think to use and that's what makes color selection such an exciting learning process.

The options—or harmonies—are monochromatic, analogous, complementary, triadic, and split complements. Within the basic harmonies shown on the wheel are many variations, factoring in light and dark versions of colors, the use of prints, solids, plaids, tone-on-tone, etc. The color wheel gives you a place to start when selecting colors.

Option #3 - The Focus Fabric

You can also use a multi-color print fabric as the basis for your color scheme, choosing your additional colors from the print. If you look carefully at the print, you will more than likely determine that the colors in the print reflect one of the possible combinations or harmonies from the color wheel.

After you've decided which color option to try, substitute your chosen colors for the areas of black or gray in your shaded design. You may find it easiest to do this by using both the shaded illustration and the line drawing. As you look at the shaded black/white illustration, find an area you can isolate and color that in with one of your selected colors on a line drawing copy of the design. Repeat this procedure for all your selected colors.

Figure 6-5

The colors in this design are all the same value. There is no contrast to delineate the separate areas of the design.

Figure 6-6

The design is colored in three values—dark yellow green, light violet, and medium yellow orange. The contrasts give the separate areas definition.

Value

The first color drawing you make may only have a single value, probably medium, of the various colors you have selected (see Figure 6-5). This will be especially true if you are a beginning quilter without much experience in selecting colors for a design.

To add interest to a design, introduce more value or contrast in lightness or darkness to the project. This means that some of the medium value areas need to be replaced with your colors in dark or light value ranges. Make your own decision whether an area should be light or dark (see Figure 6-6).

This illustration shows only three values—a dark yellow green, a light violet, and a medium yellow orange. But the values delineate separate design focus points and make the design more interesting than the version in Figure 6-5.

Texture

The second principle to consider in terms of fabrics is texture or design. You probably won't select all solid colors when you choose the fabrics for your quilt. You will probably choose tone-on-tone, plaid, floral, geometric print, and so on. A range of different textures on the fabrics will provide more visual excitement and interest for your quilt.

Once you have the general color scheme you wish to work with, select specific fabrics in those colors and play with putting them together. Select a range of values and a range of textures. It shouldn't take long to find your three or four fabrics, in several values, that work together and that reflect colors you wish to use.

Below are the steps I use when taking a design from the black/white version to the final quilt. I have selected the design from Figure 3-10 and detailed the steps used to convert it to color. Once you run through all the steps for one design, decide which steps you can eliminate to make the process quicker.

Figure 6-7

Original design

Step 1.

Begin with an original design with areas of interest illustrated in black/white.

Step 2.

Make a line drawing of the design. Consider reversing the black/white areas to see if one variation is superior to the other.

Figure 6-8

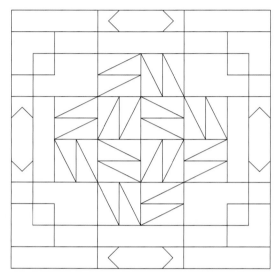

Line drawing of the design. With this, you can reverse the black/white spaces and add specific colors. When a design is reduced to only its basic lines, you can also decide to shade it in a completely different arrangement of black/white areas.

Here, shading has been added to the line drawing. The light and dark areas have been reversed. Decide which version you prefer. I selected the version in Figure 6-7.

Figure 6-9

Step 3.

Substitute two colors for the black and white. This shows how color begins to affect the design, since the contrast of colors won't be as great as the contrast between black/white (see Figure 6-9). You'll probably be able to drop this step when you understand the general technique.

Color is introduced into the quilt design. Dark blue is substituted for the black and light blue replaces the white.

Step 4.

Select a color scheme—I chose blue green, blue violet, and orange for this example. In terms of the color wheel strategy, this is a split complementary harmony. I selected different values of these colors and experimented with them in the line drawing. If you are unsure of yourself with the first project, be sure to do Step 3 with only medium values of your selected colors. Don't include the values until the second color drawing (see Figure 6-10). Choosing which colors to include in which values is not based on any particular rule of thumb. I used six values to really separate areas of the design. I wanted the design to look more complex without adding more piecework.

Step 5.

Once I saw the design in color, I made some additional modifications, specifically in the background (see Figure 6-11). I decided to use the version on the left.

Figure 6-10

The color combination of blue green, blue violet, and orange makes this harmony a split complement. Following the rule of including a variety of colors, I colored this design with six colors. There are two values of orange, one value of blue violet, and three values of blue green.

Figure 6-11

The background of the design is made more complex in these two variations. On the left, the background is broken to create a frame for the center. On the right, the background is colored with four gradations of blue green.

Step 6.

I chose actual fabrics to reflect or represent the colors in the illustration. The photograph shows the finished wall quilt.

As you can see, adding color to your design is not difficult but it is a major step in the design process. Color can make or break a good design. Color choices must be appealing and must be used to enhance and develop the design. Adding color is really fun. Quilters love all the wonderful color selections available in fabrics. You may be overwhelmed by choices, but if you follow the ideas I have presented for color selection, you will develop a new understanding of color combinations to use and try.

Remember, no system is foolproof. Be flexible. As you cut out your fabric pieces and place them together on your design wall, you may find that one fabric color just doesn't work. Go to your stash or quilt store and find a fabric that will work. Don't use a color that isn't what you want or that doesn't provide the visual impact you desire. You have spent considerable time creating your design and you will spend more time cutting, sewing, and quilting, so be sure you achieve the visual result you want.

Puzzle Pieces (47" x 47"). Designed and sewn by Joyce Mori, hand-quilted by Delores Stemple. The colorful hand-dyed fabrics look like puzzle pieces standing out against the dark blue background. Block #61 is featured.

(7" x 9"). These photos show two versions of Block #20. On the top is one featuring marbled fabric from Marble T Designs. The bottom version features an ethnic print fabric. The same block can look very different, depending on the fabrics used.

The Crooked Path (30" x 38"). The block is #44. The quilt was designed, sewn, and machine-quilted by Joyce Mori. The tiny blue print and red calico give this quilt a more traditional appearance despite the contemporary look of the block.

Chapter 7

Embellishments

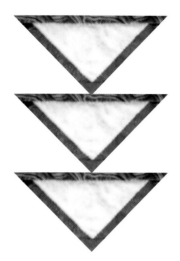

To embellish means to beautify something. An embellishment is an ornament or decoration. Quilters often look for ways to add extra beauty or decoration to their quilts and surface embellishment of quilt blocks or quilts can be a wonderful way to add pizzazz, texture, design, and/or color to the final piece. There are wonderful examples of and directions for three-dimensional appliqué, beading, fabric manipulation, embroidery, fancy buttons, pleats, and more in quilting magazines and books. Many of these techniques can be utilized in the designs you create from the designing ideas in this book. Please go to your favorite quilt store to find books that discuss the how-to of these techniques.

There is a fine line between enhancing a design with embellishments and overpowering it. Generally, the rule "less is better" should be your guide. Use embellishments sparingly until you achieve a feel for how they work in a quilt block. Perhaps you could use embellishment in some, but not all, blocks of the project. For instance, in a wall quilt with a nine-block set, you could use embellishments in the center block or in the center block and the four corner blocks.

Avoid heavy embellishments that might distort your quilt as it hangs.

Sometimes you may not really notice an embellishment until you move up close to the quilt. The embellishment then is a surprise for the viewer. An effective embellishment should read well from a distance and up close because the quilt will be seen from both distances.

I have used several very simple and easy embellishment ideas in quilt blocks pictured in this chapter. Hopefully, these ideas will inspire you to try embellishments in some of your designs.

Block #49

This block shows fabric collage in the blue triangles. Scraps of dyed blue fabric were adhered to a backing fabric with Sullivan's basting spray. Random straight line stitching was used to secure the fabric pieces to the foundation. The triangles were cut from this embellished fabric and sewn in the quilt block. Using metallic thread on the fabric collage would have provided additional highlights. When the quilt is washed, the edges of the fabric scraps will fray slightly, adding even more texture.

(12" x 12"). Block #49. Scrap pieces of blue dyed fabric were held in place with Sullivan's Quilt Basting Spray. The fabrics were stitched down and the triangle shapes cut from the resulting fabric.

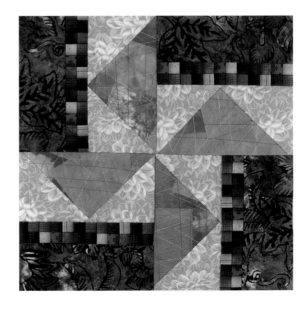

Block #19

Here a heavy chenille yarn was secured to background fabric with various colored threads. Rinse-away stabilizer was placed on top of the fabric and yarn before they were stitched down. If you use a couching foot on your sewing machine, you can omit the stabilizer and still have the yarn secured tightly to the background fabric.

(8" x 8"). Block #19. Chenille yarn was couched to the background fabric and this fabric was used in two of the rectangles. This design looks like a flower and could be colored accordingly.

Block #29 PH

One square on this block has a pleated texture, which you might not notice until you are close to the quilt. To make the pleating easy to do, I used a Perfect Pleater board and skipped every other louver. I pleated the fabric with the right side down. Once the fabric was placed in the louvers, I ironed a fusible, very lightweight interfacing onto the pleats. After this dried thoroughly, I removed it from the pleater board. Then I cut the fabric into the desired sizes and decided how to sew down and flip the pleats.

(8" x 8"). Block #29PH. A leaf fabric is pleated and placed in one of the squares of the block to add surface texture to the block.

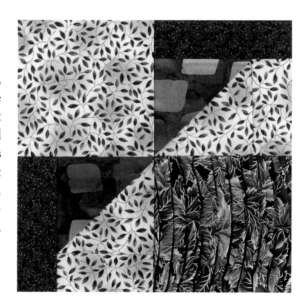

Block #12

This block has a very contemporary look. The fabric selection played an important role in the total appearance, but to reinforce the modern, abstract nature of the block, small geometric shapes in black fabric were appliquéd onto the block. This block resembles a modern art painting.

(6" x 8"). Block #12. Black geometric shapes were appliquéd randomly on the block to reinforce the contemporary theme of the print fabric.

Block #17

To help create an ethnic feeling in this block, a tribal fabric was used for the main portion of the design. Jumbo black rickrack was sewn on the corner strips to reinforce the primitive designs in the fabric and create an overall ethnic look.

(10" x 10"). In Block #17, jumbo black rickrack was used for embellishment at each corner.

Block #44

This block could be seen as very contemporary looking. In this version, silky fabrics and gold button embellishments gave the block a very formal appearance. A pink satin and a tie fabric were backed with very lightweight, fusible interfacing and the block pieces cut out. A dark floral cotton fabric with gold highlights was added to complete the fabric selection. The resulting block is not modern, but romantic looking.

(7" x 7"). Block #44 embellished with buttons and sewn with some satin and tie fabrics.

Block #3

The center rectangles of this block appear to be strip pieced, but the green strips were edged with a serger and machine sewn on top of the red print fabric. You could also fuse a narrow fabric strip on the block and use a decorative machine stitch to secure the edges.

(12" x 12"). Block #3 features serged edged strips in the center of the long rectangles in the block.

Block #55

This block is really four blocks sewn together. The dark square in each block is a piece of fabric from a broomstick skirt that was scrunched and fused to lightweight interfacing. Free motion stitching secured the bumps and lumps of the fabric. A close-up look is needed to notice this texture.

(16" x 24"). This is Block #55 and its mirror image combined into a four-block unit. A scrunch fabric is used in the center squares.

Block #48 Modified

The embellishment for this block is the center rectangle. I saved pieces of thread from my machine embroidery work and placed them on a piece of fabric and covered them with soluble stabilizer. This was heavily sewn over to secure the various threads. Once the stabilizer was rinsed away, I had this wonderful texture of swirling threads. The colors blended perfectly with the paisley fabric and the beige background.

(10" x 10"). Block #48 features a center rectangle with thread collage. Scrap pieces of thread were laid on the background fabric and soluble stabilizer placed on top. Free motion stitching was done all over the top of the stabilizer. When the stitching was complete, the fabric was placed in water and the stabilizer disappeared, leaving the collage of thread pieces.

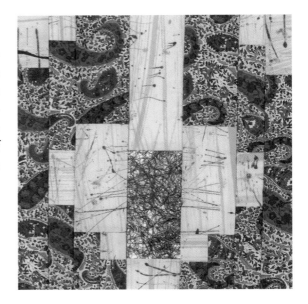

Block #57

This Native American-looking block features a very subtle embellishment. The most centered chili peppers were outline stitched with black embroidery thread. Lines of straight stitch embroidery in colors matching the peppers were also added to the body of the pepper. You can use hand- or machine-embroidery to outline any special motif on a fabric.

(10" x 12"). Block #57 has some of the chili peppers highlighted with embroidery stitches. They stand out from the other peppers in the fabric.

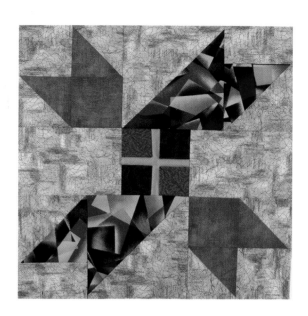

Block #45

The center square of this block has dimensional flaps placed in each corner. The flaps are from fabrics in colors found in the geometric print fabric. From a distance, the flaps look like squares that are part of a pieced block.

(16" x 16"). Block #45 features folded fabric pieces placed in the center square as dimensional embellishment pieces.

Block #2

This unit is four blocks combined. The center square of each block features a silk flower, removed from a stem of flowers, that has been fused on a background fabric. This was overlaid with organdy and outline-stitched around the outer edge of the petals.

(14" x 14"). Block #2 is repeated four times to form this design. The center of each block features a silk flower overlaid with organdy. The flower has been fused to the background and the organdy held in place by hand-stitching around the outside of the flower.

The embellishments on these blocks are not difficult. They take a little extra time but they are fun to try and add more originality to your designs.

Chapter 8

Sewing a Design

y now you have created several blocks and wall quilt designs and have selected colors and fabrics for your designs. Now you need to sew the designs. It's very simple to figure out the templates you will need and to create the piecing diagram for your designs.

I will show you how to look at individual blocks and then I will demonstrate the concepts on the larger scale of wall quilt designs. The supply list on page 9 includes a sheet of transparent 1/4" grid template plastic, which you'll use to analyze a design. Since all the design templates in this book, as well as the blocks in the gallery section, are based on the 1/4" grid, if you lay the grid template plastic over your block, you can visualize the divisions in a block.

Figure 8-1

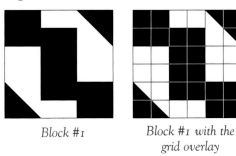

Block #1   Block #1 with the
                  grid overlay

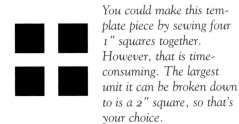

You could make this template piece by sewing four 1" squares together. However, that is time-consuming. The largest unit it can be broken down to is a 2" square, so that's your choice.

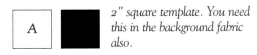

2" square template. You need this in the background fabric also.

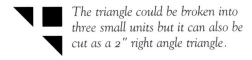

The triangle could be broken into three small units but it can also be cut as a 2" right angle triangle.

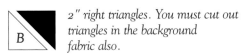

2" right triangles. You must cut out triangles in the background fabric also.

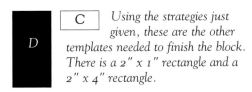

Using the strategies just given, these are the other templates needed to finish the block. There is a 2" x 1" rectangle and a 2" x 4" rectangle.

Block #1

The measurements given are the finished size. No seam allowances have been added.

First you see the block as it would appear after you created it, then as it looks with the grid template plastic placed on top of it. Each 1/4" square on the template is a possible piece to be sewn. However, you want to make your template pieces as large as possible to reduce cutting and sewing time.

For purposes of these exercises, 1/4" on the grid equals 1" in terms of the actual size you would make the template. So instead of looking at the square as four 1" templates, you need to visualize it as a 2" square. You are mentally removing some of the grid lines to have a larger template piece. The same is true for the triangle which can be broken down into two triangles and one square. The best sewing/cutting strategy is a 2" right angle triangle. You need templates in the dark fabric and the light fabric areas. Sometimes it is the same template; other times there is a new template size. To complete templates for the block you need a 2" x 4" rectangle and a 2" x 1" rectangle.

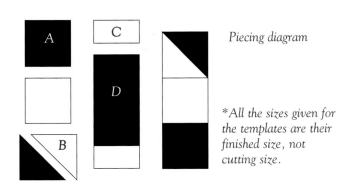

Piecing diagram

*All the sizes given for the templates are their finished size, not cutting size.

Cutting requirements for the block:

Template A - 2 dark, 2 light

Template B - 2 dark, 2 light

Template C - 2 light

Template D - 1 dark

A piecing diagram is also shown so you can see how easy it is to sew the block together. You might want to go back to your original design elements and place them on the grid surface to determine the order you would sew together the templates. Usually you group elements together to form rows and then sew the rows together. You want to avoid set-in piecing whenever possible. Quilters who have put together a number of blocks or quilts won't need to do this step because they are very familiar with the ways blocks are sewn together. There is likely more than one way a block can be put together.

Block #7

Block #7 is a slightly more complex block. Figure 8-2 shows it with and without the grid overlay and the templates necessary to complete the block.

The new twist with this block is that in two cases, the elements don't line up on the grid. You need to remember that half a grid square (1/8")

equals 1/2". Look at the piecing diagram. The finished sizes of the templates are shown on the row with the off-grid elements. Notice that this design is broken into horizontal rows. The previous block used vertical rows. You could also break this block into sections rather than rows. There is no right or wrong way. Use the system that is easiest for you to visualize, cut, and sew.

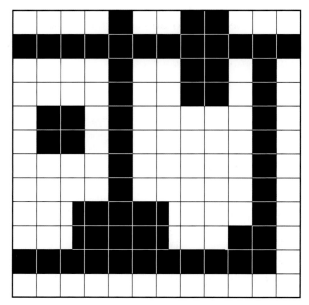

Grid overlay on top of the block

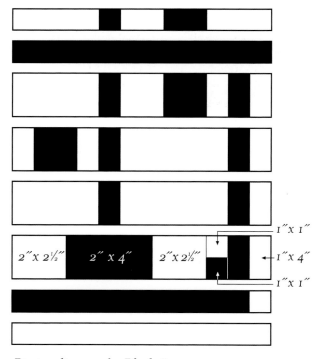

Piecing diagram for Block #7

Figure 8-2

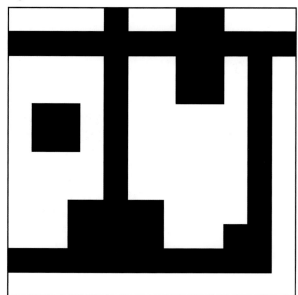

Block #7

Block #31 PH

This block, designed by Pat Hill, appears very complex when presented in black and white, but you see it is not difficult to sew together because the template pieces are fairly large. There are many pieces, making it an intermediate level block, but the sewing is straightforward. The design can be broken into horizontal or vertical rows. In Chapter 7, you learned how to do color shading so if you have worked with this block you may have already divided it into sections with colors.

Figure 8-3

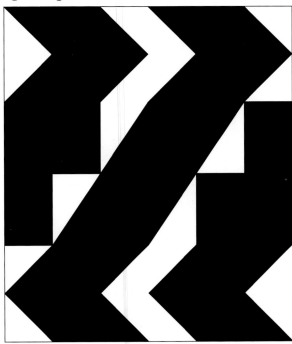

The original Block #31PH looks massive and very complex.

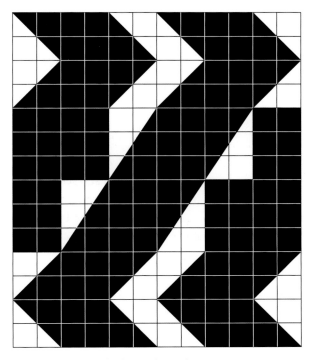

Block #31PH with the grid overlay

Color shading added to delineate some design areas

Figure 8-4

Figure 8-5

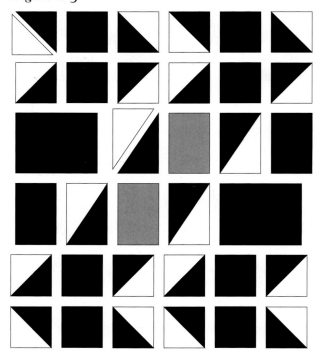

Piecing diagram for the block. Notice two of the large black areas are further subdivided to delineate more design areas.

Figure 8-4 is shown with the grid overlay. After you see the overlay in place, you can begin to visualize some of the possible units you could isolate in the block. The grid lines allow you to visualize both piecing strategies and possible new areas to delineate in the design.

You can add color to delineate design areas revealed by the grid overlay. Notice how different the two illustrations look. This shows you that blocks can usually be colored, shaded, and arranged in more than one way. The illustrations show four blocks combined. In the top version, the block was used in mirror image to create the central blue and violet section. In the bottom example, a larger area was divided to arrive at the orange rectangles with blue triangles on each side.

Remember that the grid overlay divides the block/quilt into small segments. You want to use the largest size template possible. Once you have created the templates, you can develop the easiest piecing diagram and your block is ready to sew.

The basic steps are the same for all blocks, easy or complex.

Step 1.

Place the grid overlay on top of your block design.

Step 2.

Decide on the largest cutting template pieces you can use. There may be times when you need to use the small template pieces to sew a block to avoid set-in piecing, but the general rule is to keep your template pieces as large as possible.

Step 3.

Create your piecing diagram. Go back and pull out your design template pieces to help you with this step if needed.

Step 4.

Write down the cutting requirements for your block.

Once you understand how a block is dissected for cutting and sewing, you are ready to apply those same principles to wall quilt designs. If your wall quilt is made up of nine blocks, you only have to create a piecing diagram and templates for one block. All other blocks will have the same templates. Wall quilts created in the medallion style are really treated as a large block when determining the cutting and sewing options.

Figures 8-6 and 8-7 take you through the basic steps for creating templates and a piecing diagram for a wall quilt. Here, I use Figure 3-4 reduced in scale from the original based on a 1/4" grid. You may have drawings like this also. You might have reduced the size of the illustration because you didn't want to work with larger pieces of paper and you wanted everything to fit on an 8½" x 11" piece of paper.

If you only use an 8½" x 11" grid design page, the resulting size of your wall quilt design will be limited to approximately 26" x 36", using the 1/4" equals 1" scale. You can buy large pieces of 1/4" grid graph paper that allow you to design larger quilts and stay with the 1/4" grid.

As long as you are working in the 1/4" grid, you can lay the clear plastic grid template page on top of your design or parts of the design and work out the best templates with it. But if you are working with a reduced size design, you must divide up your quilt into sections, creating template pieces. The example is not based on the 1/4" grid.

Step 1.

Mark off sections on the illustration to create workable templates. Notice that the large triangle was not broken down into smaller pieces.

Figure 8-6

Illustration with template lines marked in place

Step 2.

Create your piecing diagram.

Figure 8-7

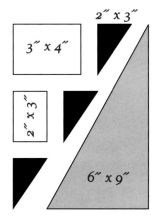

Here the templates are separated into piecing units.

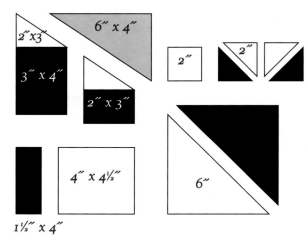

Step 3.

Since you can't use the 1/4" grid, you must figure out the size of your templates. This is not difficult. Go back to your original design pieces. Place the 1/4" clear grid over them and determine the size. In this figure, the top left unit is 6" x 9". Once you know the original size of the elements, you can ascertain the size of the templates. Your original design drawing, prior to reducing, can also be used to size templates. I have indicated the template sizes on the piecing diagram.

You now have completed the templates and piecing diagram and determined the size of the templates for the wall quilt. Follow these same steps for any reduced size drawing you may have.

Changing the Size of the Quilt

Up to this point, 1/4" on the design elements has equaled 1" on a template or quilt. That is an easy scale to use. The quilt in Figure 8-6 would be 24" x 36". If you want a larger quilt, you can change the scale and say that 1/4" on the grid equals 2" in the size of template. The same quilt would then be 48" x 72". If 1/4" equals 1½" in the template, the finished quilt would be 36" x 54". You simply draw your templates to reflect the scale you have chosen.

However, if I enlarged the quilt I might find that some of the templates were too massive. Using the top block (element) in Figure 8-6, the large triangle would normally be 6" x 9". If I double the size, it would be 12" x 18". That is a very large section of fabric, so I would divide the triangle into more units to make a more complex design.

Figure 8-8 shows two different possibilities. Other sections of the quilt would also need additional units or ways of breaking up the plain space. I have shown some ideas for dividing the large triangle. The top and bottom sections illustrate different options.

To reduce the scale of the quilt rather than enlarge it, you might need to take out some elements. However, if you utilize foundation piecing, you might not mind working with tiny template pieces. The scale you select is your choice. Just remember that you may need to alter the design by adding or reducing lines, depending on the scale you select.

Figure 8-8

If the scale for this design is enlarged to 1/4" equals 2", these are additional units I might add. Notice that the top and bottom are treated differently. To illustrate another possibility, I put in only some of the grid lines to indicate templates. The grid lines distract from the visualization of the changes.

Cutting the Templates

Whenever possible, I use a rotary cutter and plastic rulers to cut my templates. I don't like to stop and make plastic templates. However, sometimes you must make a template for unusual size pieces. I highly recommend you purchase the Easy Angle triangle templates by Sharon Hultgren. They are wonderful for many of the triangles in my design elements. Likewise, the Tri and Recs Tools by Darlene Zimmerman and Joy Hoffman are very useful. Finally, read Donna Poster's book, *Guide to Rotary Cutting*. This provides instructions for rotary cutting many geometric shapes.

I hope you have had fun designing and creating your own quilt and block designs. I look forward to seeing your projects hanging in quilt shows and featured in magazines.

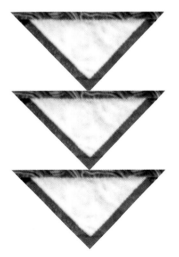

Excitement (44" x 44"). Quilt designed, sewn, and hand-quilted by Joyce Mori. The quilt block used is #33AP designed by Anastasia Pavlovic. Sixteen blocks were used for the center of the quilt. Corner pinwheels in the border were made by adding additional blue and orange triangles. Fabrics were supplied by RJR fabrics and are from the Basic Realities and Marble Montage collections.

Folk Art Arrows (35" x 35"). Designed, sewn, and hand-quilted by Joyce Mori. This quilt uses an arrow design element as a block. The quilt features fabrics in lovely folk art colors by RJR from the Basic Realities and Paint Box Prints collections.

A Frank Lloyd Wright Look-a-Like (30½" x 42"). Designed, sewn, and machine-quilted by Joyce Mori. Block #13 was turned upside-down in the center row. The overall design reminds me of the geometric window designs of Frank Lloyd Wright, though an ethnic print fabric was used in the quilt.

Chapter 9

Final Comments

Design Games

If you have enjoyed the designing process in this book, there are a few art/puzzle games that might interest you. Some of these are pricey, and others are very inexpensive. They are all based on the same principle as my design method, taking pieces and moving them around on a surface to create a design.

The pieces of these games are sometimes larger and thicker than the cardboard design element pieces in my design system. That can make them more suitable for children or for taking on trips.

Colorforms™. The puzzle consists of thin colored plastic pieces (red, yellow, and blue) in the shape of squares, rectangles, circles, and triangles. You place them on a hard plastic surface to which they adhere. They can be picked up and repositioned anywhere on the plastic coated cardboard surface. These are available in small sets and larger, more expensive sets.

Fractiles™. Seven plastic magnetic pieces in three colors can be moved around on the board to create shapes. However, all the pieces are based on a circle being divided into seven parts, so there are no squares, rectangles, or right angle triangles. The design shapes include diamonds with varying angles. These shapes are not those most often used

by quilters, but designing with these pieces would allow you to create some really lovely kaleidoscope designs.

Triangles. I don't know the name of this puzzle. It was something I found in one of those stores where everything costs a dollar. It consists of a black plastic board with a grid. Each square of the grid holds two right angle triangles. The triangles are colored in a range of bright, neon colors. This is a lot of fun because you can leave spaces on the grid empty and the black surface forms the background color. If you like cutting and sewing triangles to create quilts, this puzzle might be for you.

Tangrams. There are many companies that have tangram pieces and accompanying booklets that show possible designs that can be created. Some of them can certainly be adapted for quilt blocks.

Shape by Shape™. This is a more deluxe version of the tangrams. The thick, hard plastic pieces come in a carrying case with a set of cards to show you different designs. The plastic pieces are colored yellow and orange, but they act visually as dark/light units.

IQ Creator. Eight thick, geometric pieces can be arranged in different ways to fit into a square space. There are 48 possible combinations. You could easily modify the designs to develop quilt blocks.

Brain Boggler. This game is similar to the previous one except there are 12 different geometric shapes in black and white that fit into a rectangle. You could combine only two or three of the elements to create a possible block design. The resulting figure might not be a perfect square, it would be up to you to add additional background space to create a square. Because of the nature of the geometric shapes in these last two puzzles, you could create some very contemporary quilt blocks.

Izzi™. There are 64 designed square tiles that can be combined in many different ways. The tiles are colored in black and white. The puzzle makers want you to solve the puzzle by having black units touch only black units and white units touch white units, but you can use them any way you wish. This is a good puzzle to take on a trip and use with your

children to entice them to become interested in designing.

Nearly Almost Perhaps Impossible Puzzle™. There are four hard plastic cubes that are plain or divided into triangles. You can match them up any way you wish to create a design. The units are colored pink, purple, and yellow, which is a little distracting. But if you create something interesting, you can go back to your black/white design elements in this book and re-create it and develop it further.

Tantalizing Triangles. This puzzle has 72 equilateral triangle pieces in green, blue, yellow, and red. There are three sizes of triangles. If you enjoy working with equilateral triangle designs, this game is perfect. Hard plastic triangle templates used with a rotary cutter make cutting such shapes very easy.

If you are looking for some different designing strategies, you might consider purchasing one of these puzzles. The puzzles are to be considered a designing option. Take any designs you create with the puzzles and apply the additional options discussed in the chapters of this book to refine your ideas.

Study pictures of quilts in books, magazines, and at shows. Ask yourself why you like or dislike certain ones. Look for new design strategies or options that you can use with your designs.

Reproduce a block you like using the design elements in this book. Manipulating and moving the elements allows you to quickly try changes to the design. You can often easily develop unique new designs by playing with the very same elements used by someone else.

Start simple and progress to more complex designs. Maturation in life comes slowly, it will probably come slowly in the design process also. Most of us can't create a smashing design with the first try. But with the techniques you've now mastered, I believe you will enjoy creating original designs and sewing them into quilts. You will have a wonderful sense of satisfaction as you realize that you can be successful in designing and creating original blocks and quilts.

About the Author

Joyce Mori is the author of 11 books on quilting subjects, including *Dye It, Paint It, Quilt It* and *The Ultimate Scrap Quilt* published by Krause Publications. She has also written over 60 articles on quilting subjects.

Joyce has a Ph.D. in anthropology from the University of Missouri where she majored in Native American cultures. She keeps a data base on quilts with Native American designs. She markets quilting stencils featuring Native American designs through Quilting Creations International.

Joyce exhibits and sells her quilts and is a juried artisan in the West Virginia Parkways system. She offers lectures and workshops on various topics. She has a grown daughter and lives with her husband John in Morgantown, West Virginia.

Appendix

Gallery of Blocks

All blocks are sized to the design elements provided in the Appendix. In the text, some of the blocks had to be reduced in size because of space considerations. All blocks have a number for identification. Some of the blocks are created by guest designers—Pat Hill (PH), Theresa Fleming (TF), and Anastasia Pavlovic (AP). Their blocks are identified with a number and their initials. I created all blocks without identifying letters. You may use any of these blocks in your quilts as long as you credit the designer.

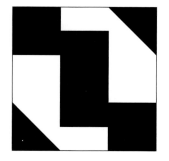

6" x 6" Block #1

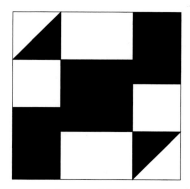

7" x 7" Block #2

12" x 12" Block #3

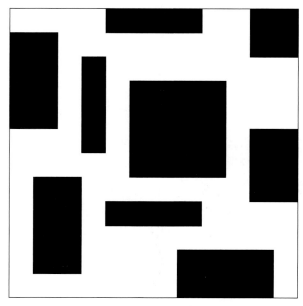

12" x 12" Block #4

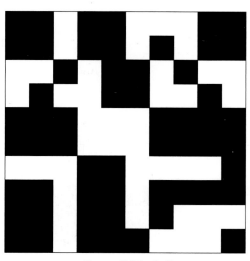

10" x 10" Block #5

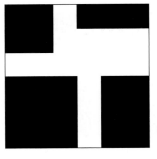

6" x 6" Block #6

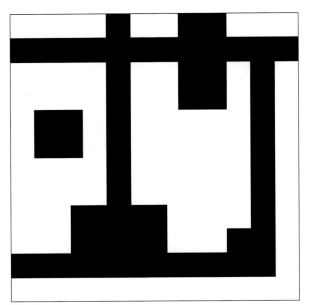

6" x 6" Block #9

12" x 12" Block #7

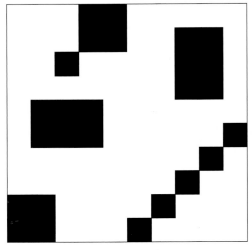

10" x 10" Block #8

12" x 12" Block #10

12" x 12" Block #11

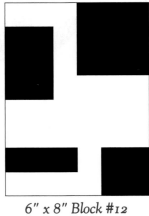

6" x 8" Block #12

4" x 8" Block #13

12" x 12" Block #14

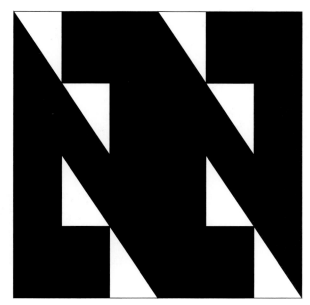

12" x 12" Block #15

10" x 10" Block #16

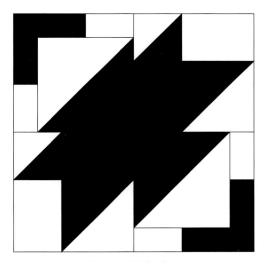

10" x 10" Block #17

8" x 10" Block #18

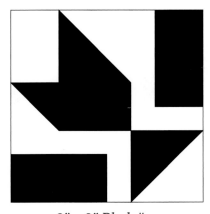

8" x 8" Block #19

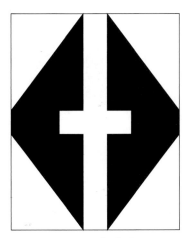

7" x 9" Block #20

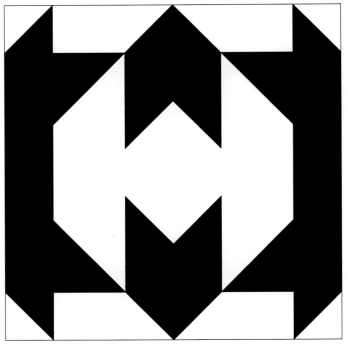

14" x 14" Block #21

10" x 10" Block #22

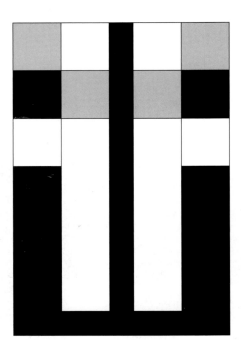

9" x 13" Block #23

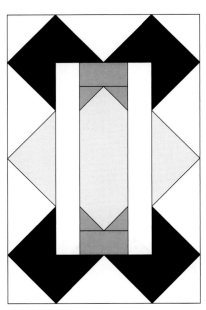

8" x 12" Block #24

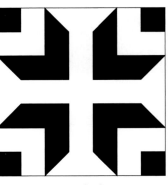

7" x 7" Block #25

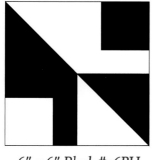

6" x 6" Block #26PH

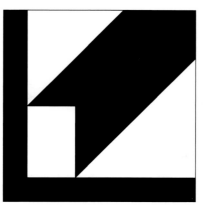

8" x 8" Block #27PH

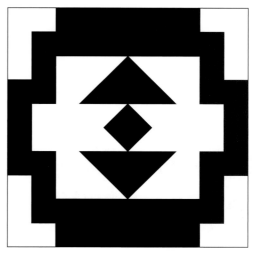

10" x 10" Block #28PH

15" x 16" Block #32PH

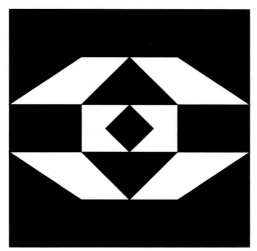

10" x 10" Block #31PH

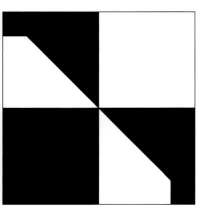

8" x 8" Block #29PH

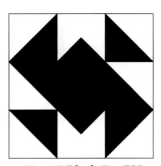

6" x 6" Block #30PH

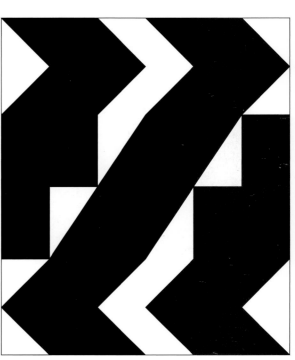

12" x 14" Block #31PH

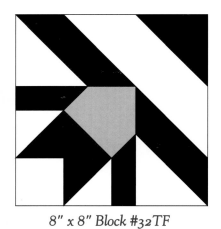

8" x 8" Block #32TF

6" x 6" Block #33AP

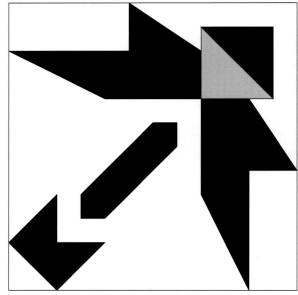

12" x 12" Block #34TF

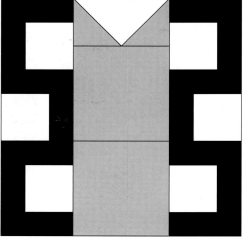

10" x 10" Block #35AP

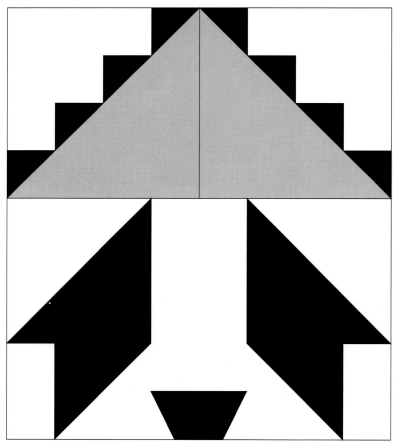

16" x 18" Block #37AP

8" x 8" Block #36AP

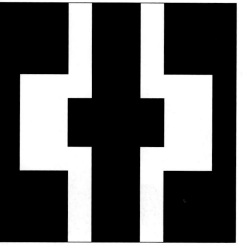

8" x 10" Block #39

10" x 10" Block #38

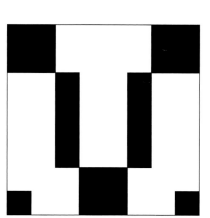

8" x 8" Block #40

8" x 8" Block #41

11" x 16" Block #42

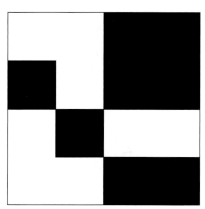

8" x 8" Block #44

14" x 14" Block #43

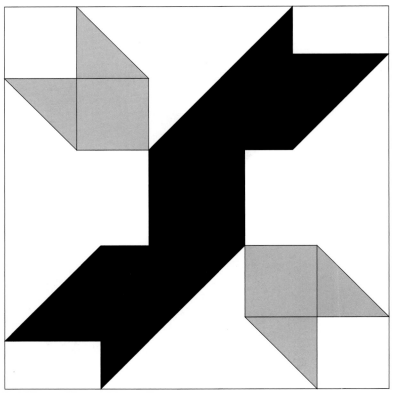

16" x 16" Block #45

12" x 20" Block #46

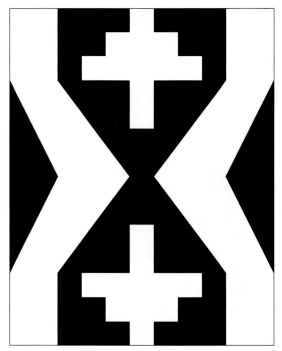

11" x 14" Block #47

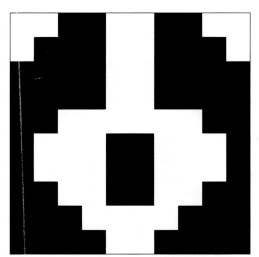

10" x 10" Block #48

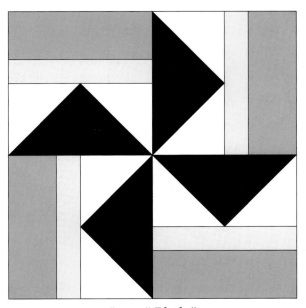

12" x 12" Block #49

10" x 10" Block #50

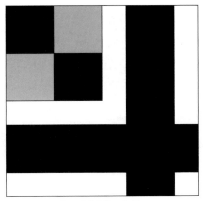

8" x 8" Block #51

12" x 12" Block #52

12" x 12" Block #53

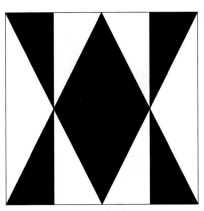

8" x 8" Block #54

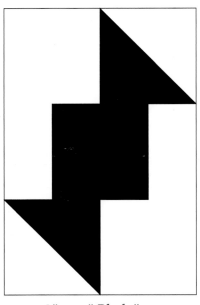

8" x 12" Block #55

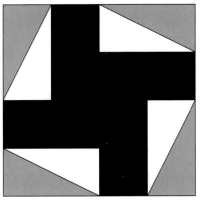

8" x 8" Block #56

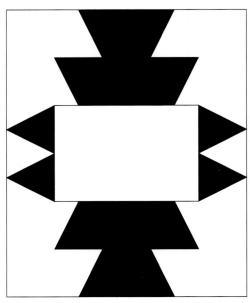

10" x 12" Block #57

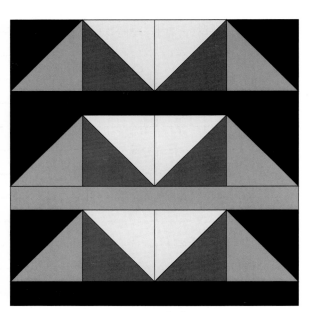

12" x 12" Block #58

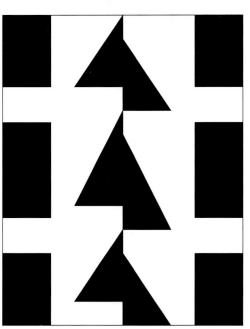

10" x 13" Block #60

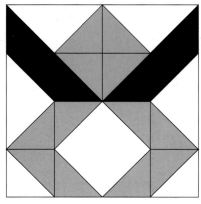

8" x 8" Block #59

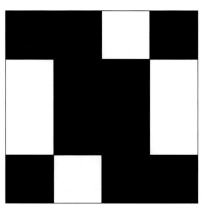

8" x 8" Block #61

Grid Page and Block Grid Pages

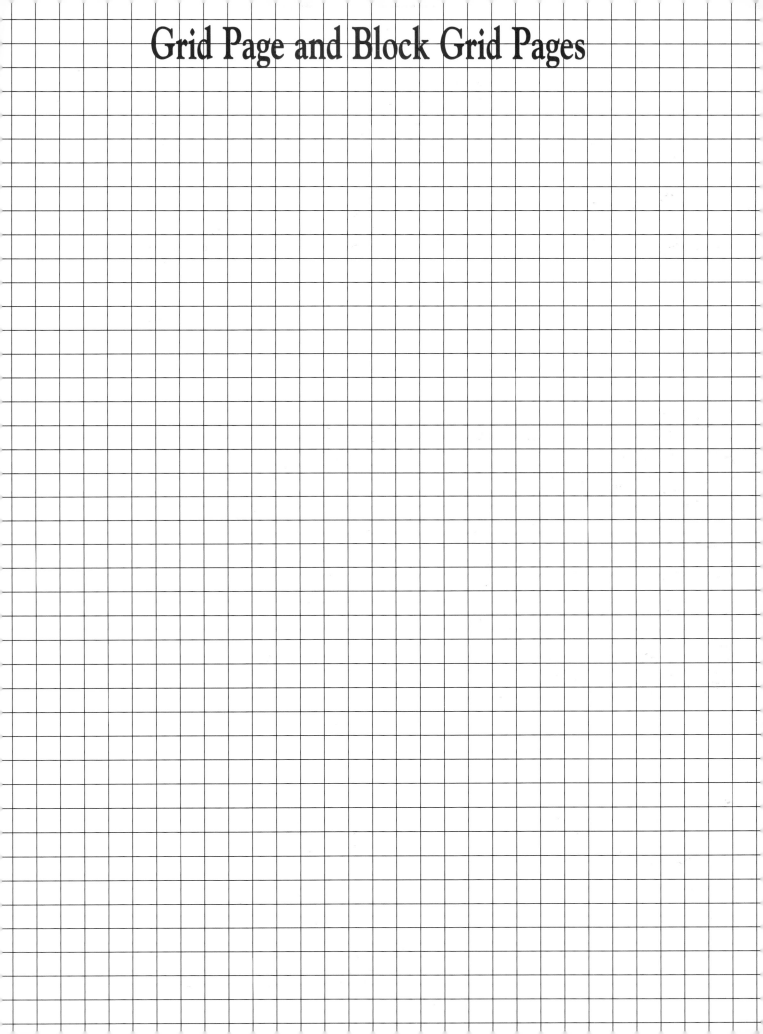

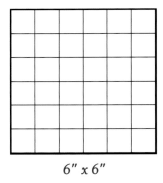

6" x 6"

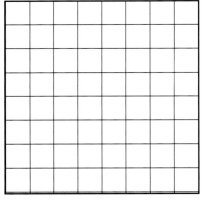

8" x 8"

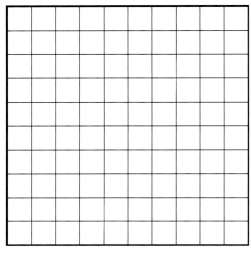

10" x 10"

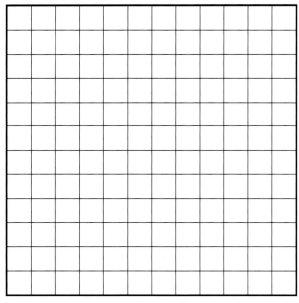

12" x 12"

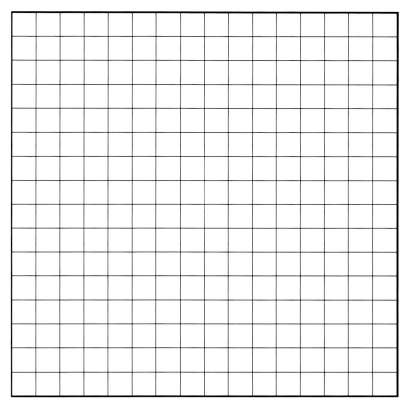

16" x 16"

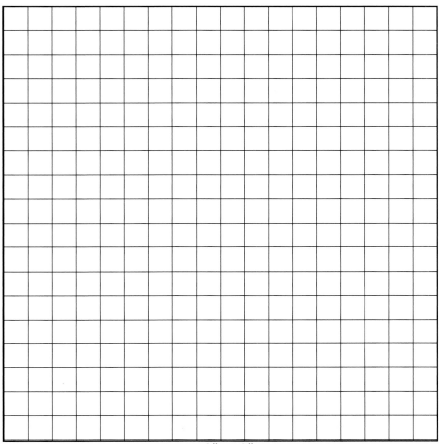

18" x 18"

Design Element Sheets

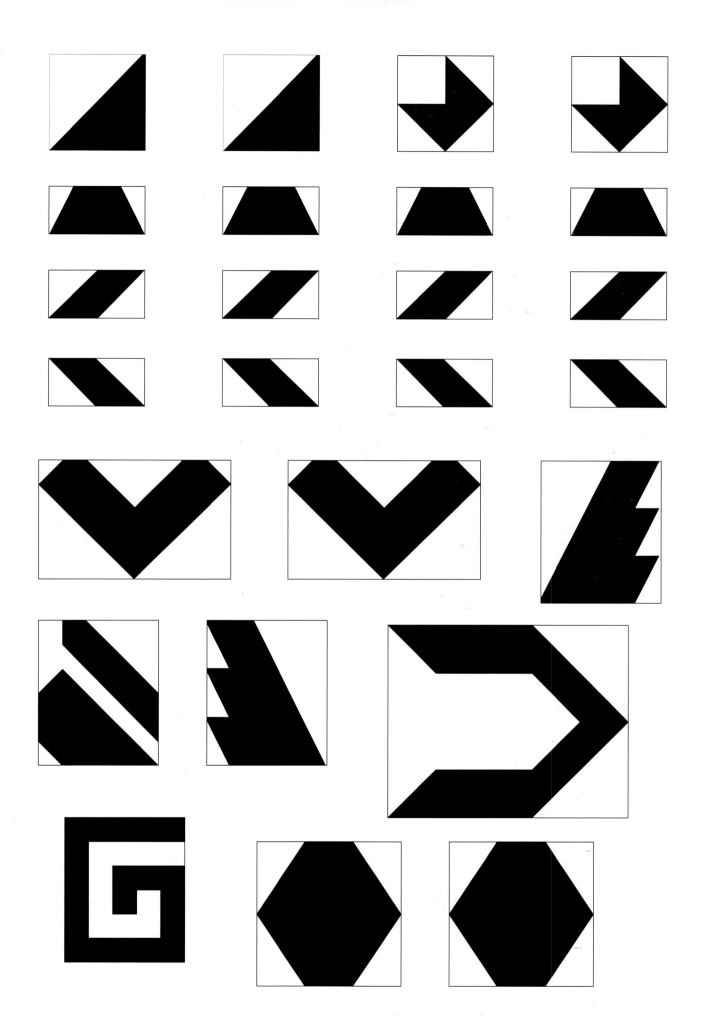

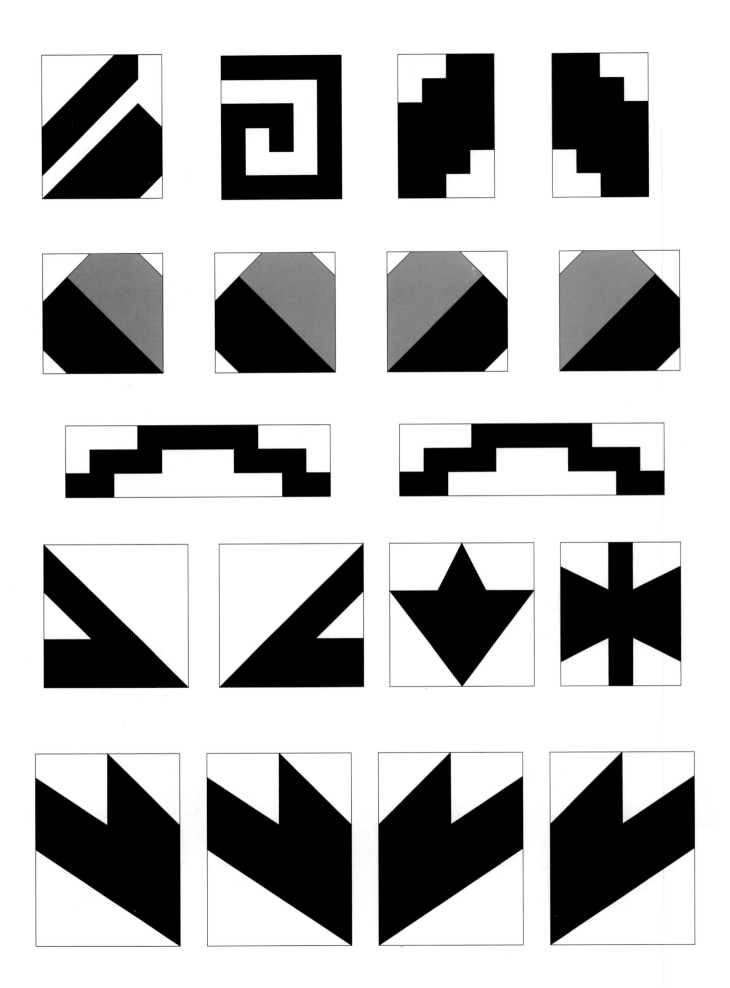

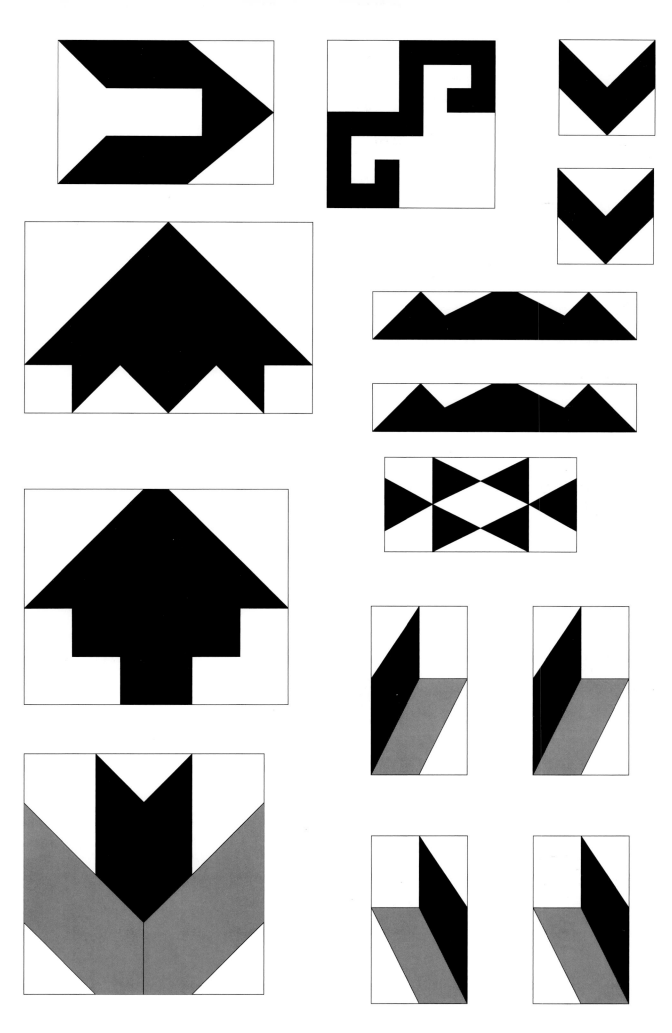

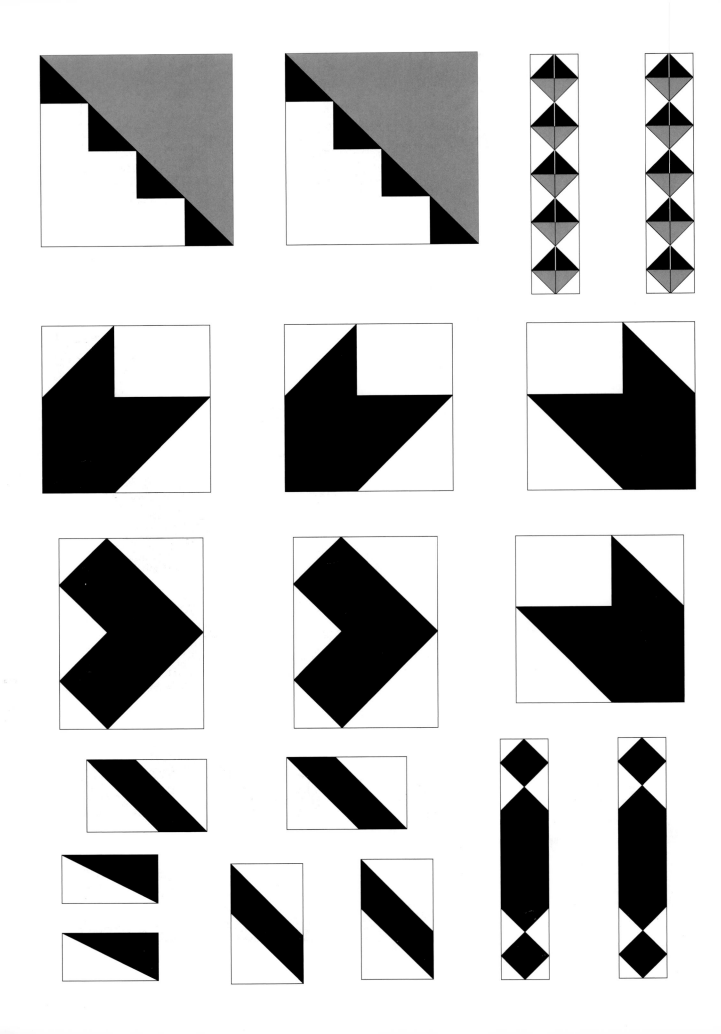

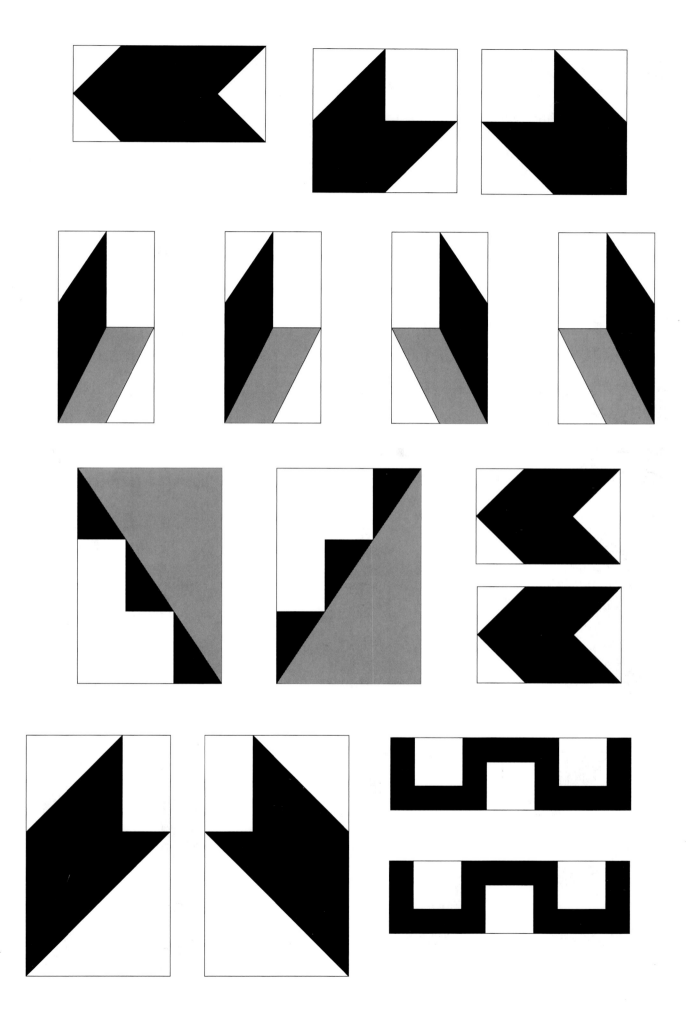

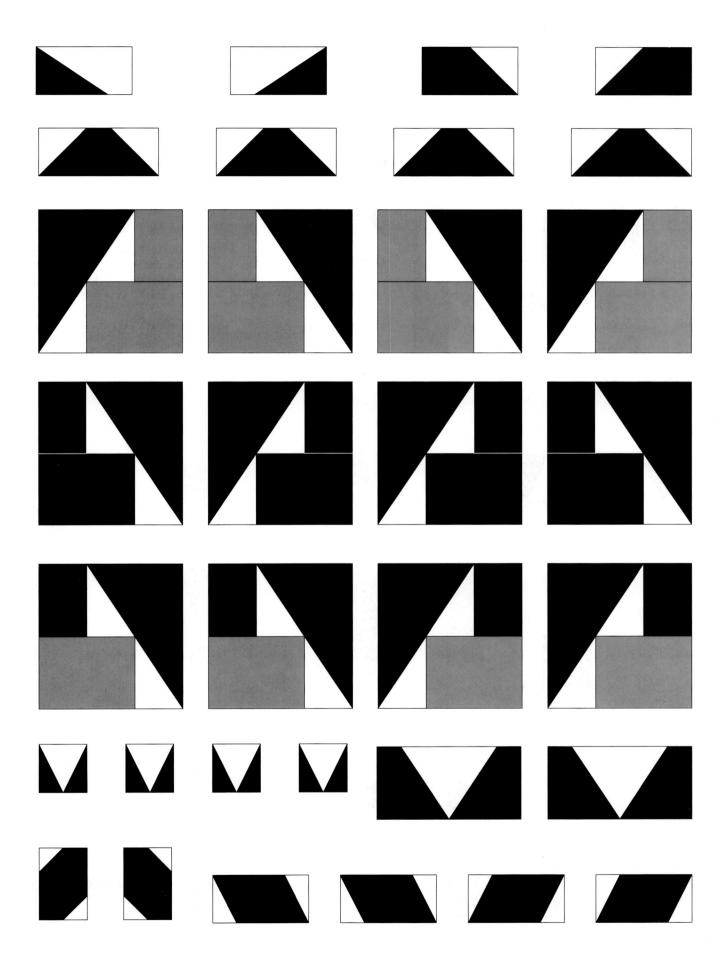

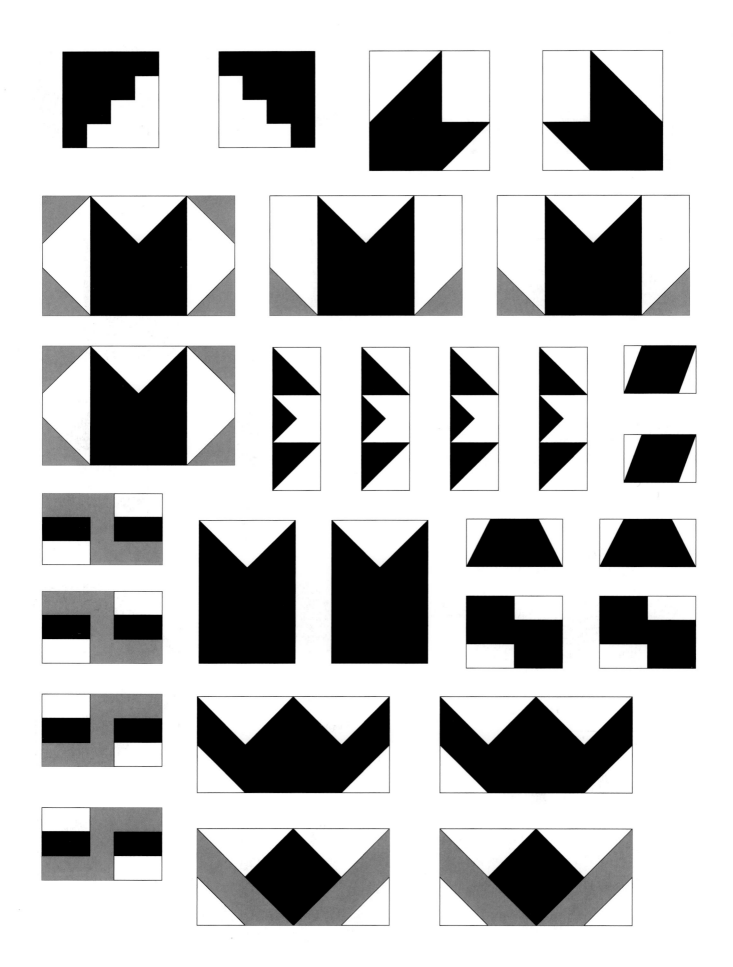

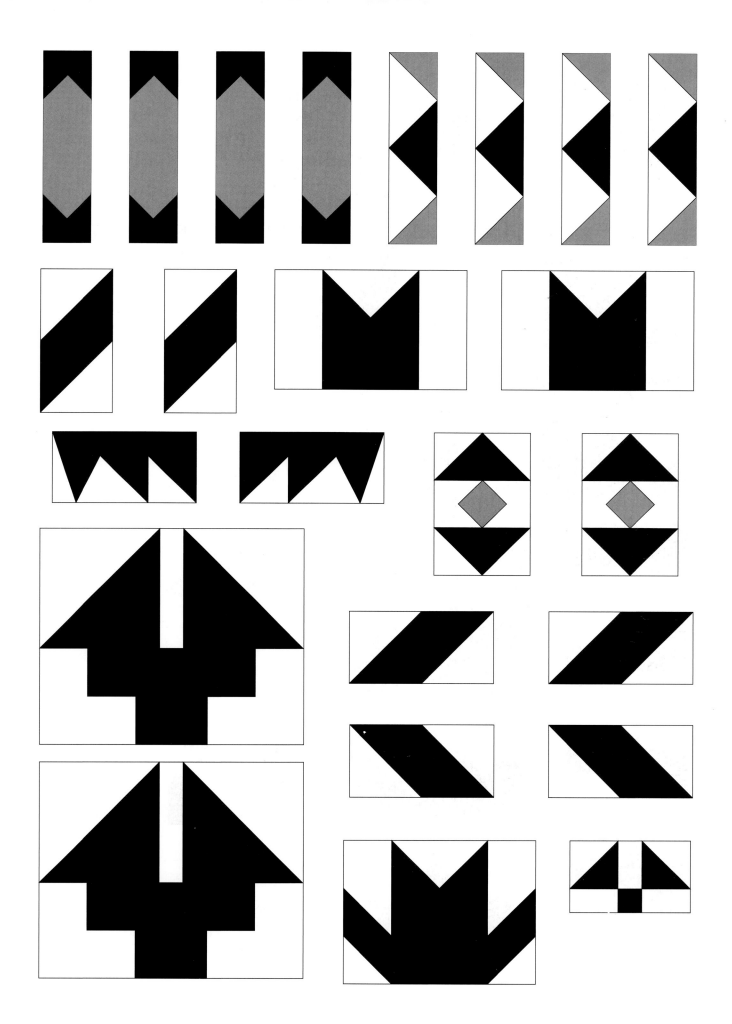

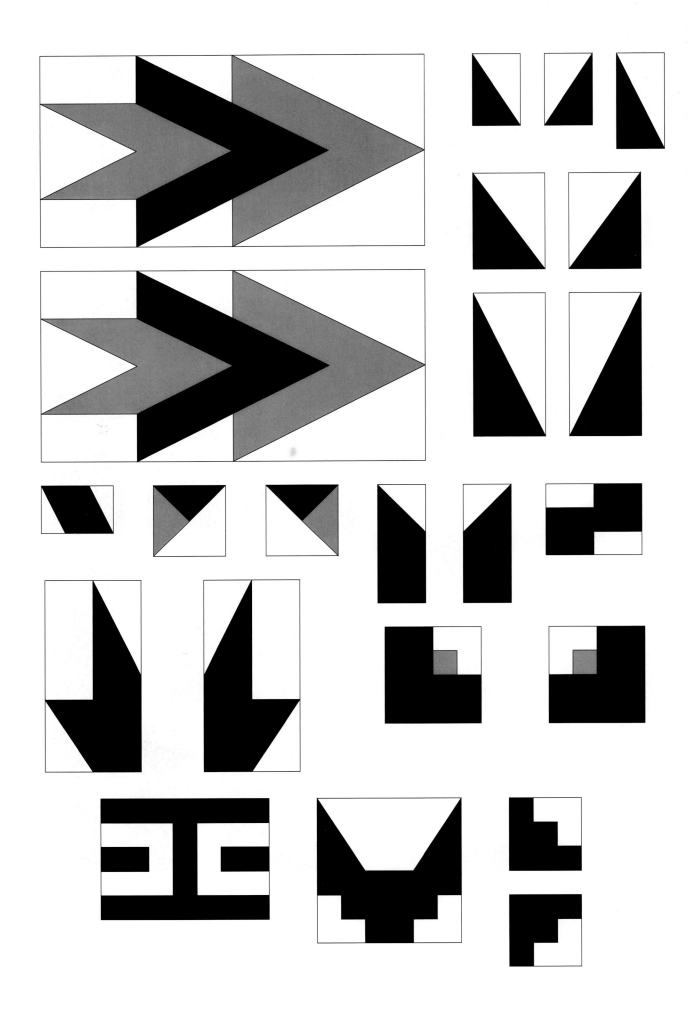

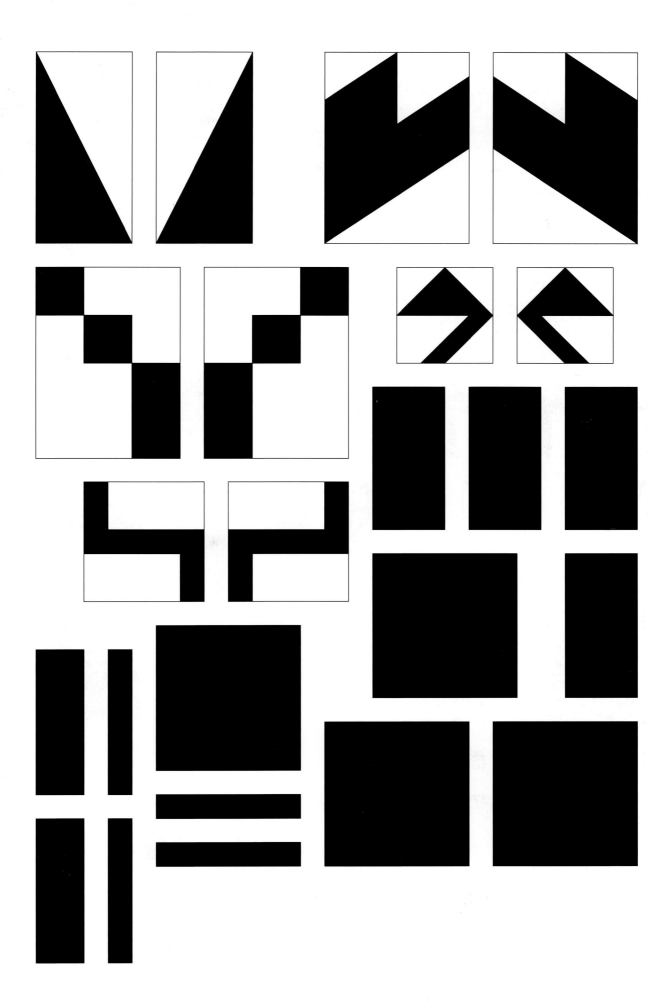

Design Element Sheets Without Shading